W9-BHA-585

THE
CIVIL WAR
A NATION DIVIDED

African Americans
and the Civil War

THE CIVIL WAR
A NATION DIVIDED

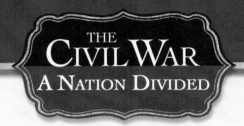

THE CIVIL WAR
A NATION DIVIDED

African Americans
and the Civil War

Ronald A. Reis / Consulting Editor **Tim McNeese**

CHELSEA HOUSE
PUBLISHERS
An imprint of Infobase Publishing

AFRICAN AMERICANS AND THE CIVIL WAR

Copyright © 2009 by Infobase Publishing

All rights reserved. No part of this book may be reproduced or utilized in any form or by any means, electronic or mechanical, including photocopying, recording, or by any information storage or retrieval systems, without permission in writing from the publisher. For information, contact:

Chelsea House
An imprint of Infobase Publishing
132 West 31st Street
New York, NY 10001

Library of Congress Cataloging-in-Publication Data
Reis, Ronald A.
  African Americans and the Civil War / by Ronald A. Reis.
     p. cm. — (The Civil War : a nation divided)
  Includes bibliographical references and index.
  ISBN 978-1-60413-038-6 (hardcover)
   1. United States—History—Civil War, 1861-1865—African Americans. 2. United States—History—Civil War, 1861-1865—Participation, African American. 3. United States. Army—African American troops—History—19th century. 4. African American soldiers—History—19th century. I. Title.

  E540.N3R46 2009
  973.7'415—dc22   2008025665

Chelsea House books are available at special discounts when purchased in bulk quantities for businesses, associations, institutions, or sales promotions. Please call our Special Sales Department in New York at (212) 967-8800 or (800) 322-8755.

You can find Chelsea House on the World Wide Web at
http://www.chelseahouse.com

Series design by Lina Farinella
Cover design by Takeshi Takahashi
Composition by North Market Street Graphics
Cover printed by Bang Printing, Brainerd, MN
Book printed and bound by Bang Printing, Brainerd, MN
Date printed: June, 2010
Printed in the United States of America

10 9 8 7 6 5 4 3 2

This book is printed on acid-free paper.

All links and Web addresses were checked and verified to be correct at the time of publication. Because of the dynamic nature of the Web, some addresses and links may have changed since publication and may no longer be valid.

Contents

Chronology

1820   The Missouri Compromise allows Maine to be admitted to the Union as a free state and Missouri as a slave state in 1821.

1831   William Lloyd Garrison publishes the first issue of his abolitionist newspaper, *The Liberator*.

1836   The House of Representatives passes a gag rule that automatically tables or postpones action on all petitions relating to slavery without hearing them.

1838   The Underground Railroad is formally organized.

1845   Former slave Frederick Douglass publishes his autobiography, *Narrative of the Life of Frederick Douglass, An American Slave*.

1850   Congress enacts several measures that together make up the Compromise of 1850.

1852   Harriet Beecher Stowe publishes *Uncle Tom's Cabin*.

1854   Congress passes the Kansas-Nebraska Act, which overturns the Missouri Compromise and thus opens northern territories to slavery.

1855   As Kansas prepares to vote, thousands of Border Ruffians from Missouri enter the territory in an attempt to influence the elections. This begins the period known as Bleeding Kansas.

1856   South Carolina representative Preston Brooks attacks Massachusetts senator Charles Sumner on the Senate floor and beats him with a cane.

1857   The Supreme Court rules, in *Dred Scott v. Sandford,* that blacks are not U.S. citizens and slaveholders have the right to take slaves into free areas of the country.

1859   John Brown seizes the arsenal at Harpers Ferry, Virginia. Robert E. Lee, then a Federal Army regular, leads the troops that capture Brown.

1860   **NOVEMBER**   Abraham Lincoln is elected president.

         DECEMBER   A South Carolina convention passes an ordinance of secession, and the state secedes from the Union.

1861   **JANUARY**   Florida, Alabama, Georgia, and Louisiana secede from the Union.

         FEBRUARY   Texas votes to secede from the Union. The Confederate States of America is formed and elects Jefferson Davis as its president.

         MARCH   Abraham Lincoln is sworn in as the sixteenth president of the United States and delivers his first inaugural address.

         APRIL 12   At 4:30 A.M., Confederate forces fire on South Carolina's Fort Sumter. The Civil War begins. Virginia secedes from the Union five days later.

         MAY   Arkansas and North Carolina secede from the Union.

         JUNE   Tennessee secedes from the Union.

         JULY 21   The Union suffers a defeat in northern Virginia, at the First Battle of Bull Run (Manassas).

         AUGUST   The Confederates win the Battle of Wilson's Creek, in Missouri.

1862   **FEBRUARY 6**   In Tennessee, Union general Ulysses S. Grant captures Fort Henry. Ten days later, he captures Fort Donelson.

MARCH The Confederate ironclad ship CSS *Virginia* (formerly the USS *Merrimack*) battles the Union ironclad *Monitor* to a draw. The Union's Peninsular Campaign begins in Virginia.

APRIL 6–7 Ulysses S. Grant defeats Confederate forces in the Battle of Shiloh (Pittsburg Landing), in Tennessee.

APRIL 24 David Farragut moves his fleet of Union Navy vessels up the Mississippi River to take New Orleans.

MAY 31 The Battle of Seven Pines (Fair Oaks) takes place in Virginia.

JUNE 1 Robert E. Lee assumes command of the Army of Northern Virginia.

JUNE 25–JULY 1 The Seven Days Battles are fought in Virginia.

AUGUST 29–30 The Union is defeated at the Second Battle of Bull Run.

SEPTEMBER 17 The bloodiest day in U.S. military history: Confederate forces under Robert E. Lee are stopped at Antietam, Maryland, by Union forces under George B. McClellan.

SEPTEMBER 22 The first Emancipation Proclamation to free slaves in the rebellious states is issued by President Lincoln.

DECEMBER 13 The Union's Army of the Potomac, under Ambrose Burnside, suffers a costly defeat at Fredericksburg, Virginia.

1863 **JANUARY 1** President Lincoln issues the final Emancipation Proclamation.

JANUARY 29 Ulysses S. Grant is placed in command of the Army of the West, with orders to capture Vicksburg, Mississippi.

MAY 1–4   Union forces under Joseph Hooker are defeated decisively by Robert E. Lee's much smaller forces at the Battle of Chancellorsville, in Virginia.

MAY 10   The South suffers a huge blow as General Thomas "Stonewall" Jackson dies from wounds he received during the battle of Chancellorsville.

JUNE 3   Robert E. Lee launches his second invasion of the North; he heads into Pennsylvania with 75,000 Confederate troops.

JULY 1–3   The tide of war turns against the South as the Confederates are defeated at the Battle of Gettysburg in Pennsylvania.

JULY 4   Vicksburg, the last Confederate stronghold on the Mississippi River, surrenders to Ulysses S. Grant after a six-week siege.

JULY 13–16   Antidraft riots rip through New York City.

JULY 18   The black Massachusetts 54th Infantry Regiment under Colonel Robert Gould Shaw assaults a fortified Confederate position at Fort Wagner, South Carolina.

SEPTEMBER 19–20   A decisive Confederate victory takes place at Chickamauga, Tennessee.

NOVEMBER 19   President Lincoln delivers the Gettysburg Address.

NOVEMBER 23–25   Ulysses S. Grant's Union forces win an important victory at the Battle of Chattanooga, in Tennessee.

1864   **MARCH 9**   President Lincoln names Ulysses S. Grant general-in-chief of all the armies of the United States.

MAY 4   Ulysses S. Grant opens a massive, coordinated campaign against Robert E. Lee's Confederate armies in Virginia.

MAY 5–6   The Battle of the Wilderness is fought in Virginia.

MAY 8–12   The Battle of Spotsylvania is fought in Virginia.

JUNE 1–3   The Battle of Cold Harbor is fought in Virginia.

JUNE 15   Union forces miss an opportunity to capture Petersburg, Virginia; this results in a nine-month Union siege of the city.

SEPTEMBER 2   Atlanta, Georgia, is captured by Union forces led by William Tecumseh Sherman.

OCTOBER 19   Union general Philip H. Sheridan wins a decisive victory over Confederate general Jubal Early in the Shenandoah Valley of Virginia.

NOVEMBER 8   Abraham Lincoln is reelected president, defeating Democratic challenger George B. McClellan.

NOVEMBER 15   General William T. Sherman begins his March to the Sea from Atlanta.

DECEMBER 15–16   Confederate general John Bell Hood is defeated at Nashville, Tennessee, by Union forces under George H. Thomas.

DECEMBER 21   General Sherman reaches Savannah, Georgia; he leaves behind a path of destruction 300 miles long and 60 miles wide from Atlanta to the sea.

1865   Southern states begin to pass Black Codes.

JANUARY 31   The U.S. Congress approves the Thirteenth Amendment to the United States Constitution.

FEBRUARY 3   A peace conference takes place as President Lincoln meets with Confederate Vice President Alexander Stephens at Hampton Roads, Virginia; the meeting ends in failure, and the war continues.

MARCH 4   Lincoln delivers his second inaugural address ("With Malice Toward None"). Congress establishes the Freedmen's Bureau.

MARCH 25   Robert E. Lee's Army of Northern Virginia begins its last offensive with an attack on the center of

Ulysses S. Grant's forces at Petersburg, Virginia. Four hours later, Lee's attack is broken.

APRIL 2　Grant's forces begin a general advance and break through Lee's lines at Petersburg. Lee evacuates Petersburg. Richmond, Virginia, the Confederate capital, is evacuated.

APRIL 9　Robert E. Lee surrenders his Confederate Army to Ulysses S. Grant at the village of Appomattox Court House, Virginia.

APRIL 14　John Wilkes Booth shoots President Lincoln at Ford's Theatre in Washington, D.C.

APRIL 15　President Abraham Lincoln dies. Vice President Andrew Johnson assumes the presidency.

APRIL 18　Confederate general Joseph E. Johnston surrenders to Union general William T. Sherman in North Carolina.

APRIL 26　John Wilkes Booth is shot and killed in a tobacco barn in Virginia.

DECEMBER　The Thirteenth Amendment is ratified.

1866　Congress approves the Fourteenth Amendment to the Constitution.

Congress passes the Civil Rights Act.

The responsibilities and powers of the Freedmen's Bureau are expanded by Congress. The legislation is vetoed by President Johnson, but Congress overrides his veto.

The Ku Klux Klan is established in Tennessee.

1867　Congress passes the Military Reconstruction Act.

Congress passes the Tenure of Office Act.

1868　The impeachment trial of President Andrew Johnson ends in acquittal.

Ulysses S. Grant is elected president.

1869　Congress approves the Fifteenth Amendment to the Constitution.

1871   The Ku Klux Klan Act is passed by Congress.

1872   President Grant is reelected.

1875   A new Civil Rights Act is passed.

1877   Rutherford B. Hayes assumes the presidency.
        The Reconstruction Era ends.

Masters and Slaves

Solomon Bradley, 27 years old in 1863, was a black mechanic living and working as a slave on the railroad between Charleston and Savannah. One morning he went for a drink of water at a house near the railroad line. The home was at the center of a large plantation, owned by a man named Farrarby. Upon approaching the dooryard, Bradley's ears were pierced by the most dreadful howling, screaming, and crying he had ever heard. Looking through an opening in the board fence, Bradley saw a woman stretched on the ground, face downward, her hands and feet bound to stakes. Her master, Farrarby, stood over her and was striking her with a leather trace belonging to his carriage harness. "As the strokes fell, the flesh of her back and legs was raised in welts and ridges," Bradley would tell the American Freedmen's Inquiry Commission. "Occasionally, when the poor creature cried out with insufferable pain, her tormentor kicked her in the mouth to silence her."

According to Bradley, when Farrarby had exhausted himself from flogging, he called for sealing wax and a lighted candle. The slave driver melted the wax and dropped it on the woman's injured back. Then, taking a riding whip and standing over the poor woman, Farrarby deliberately switched off the hardened wax with his whip. As this scene of torture was acted out, Farrarby's grown-up daughters looked on from a window that opened on the yard.

Soon afterward, Bradley sought to find out what terrible offense the woman had committed to draw such harsh punishment. Her fellow servants told him that the woman's only crime was burning the edges of the waffles that she had cooked for breakfast. Bradley was overcome with grief and despair by what he had witnessed. "The sight of the thing made me wild, and I could not work right that day," he bemoaned. "I prayed the Lord to help my people out of their bondage."

African Americans would eventually come out of bondage, another word for slavery. Close to 4 million were living in bondage at the time of the Civil War, 1861 to 1865. In the process of gaining freedom for African Americans, 620,000 Americans would lose their lives, the greatest loss in any American war, before or since. In the Civil War, African Americans did not stand by idly, passively waiting for Northern liberators to destroy slavery and set them free. More than 200,000 blacks served in the Union army and navy. Nearly 37,000 of them died fighting for their liberty and the restoration of the Union.

There were many battles where black soldiers, enlisted by the Bureau of Colored Troops, fought bravely in defeat as well as in victory. Both free African Americans and runaway slaves joined in the fight. At first, there were whites, especially in the North, who thought that blacks would not or could not fight for their freedom. It was assumed that, as Benjamin Quarles declared in *The Negro in the Civil War,* "The Negro was too grossly ignorant to perform the duties of a soldier intelligently, and that blacks were not fit to wear a military uniform because they belonged to a degraded, inferior race, lacking in manly qualities."

On the battlefield and on the home front, African Americans would prove such critics wrong. In spite of gross prejudice, outright racism, and the unfulfilled promise of full equality, blacks made a significant, perhaps key, contribution to the Union triumph in the Civil War. Indeed, to President Abraham Lincoln, African-American troops, as quoted in *The Negro's Civil War*, " . . . made the difference between victory and defeat."

TRAFFICKING IN HUMAN FLESH

More than 50 years before Christopher Columbus set sail in 1492, Portuguese sailors traveled south to the west coast of Africa. They went as explorers, curious as to what treasures they might find or what routes, if any, were possible around the Muslim-controlled southern Mediterranean. Gold dust and ivory were soon discovered and traded for rum, cloth, guns, and other goods. In 1442, however, a Portuguese ship returned to Europe with more than shiny metal and tusks: It arrived with a cargo of 10 Africans. Thus began three and a half centuries of slave trading that would witness, according to the American Freedmen's Inquiry Commission, "Upward of fifteen million and a half of human beings forcibly torn from their native country, and doomed to perpetual slavery—themselves and their offspring—in a foreign land."

Europeans were aided in their slave trading by more than a few Africans willing to supply human cargo in exchange for guns, mirrors, and the like. The most obvious labor source came from prisoners of war. According to Major General Rooke, as quoted in the American Freedmen's Inquiry Commission report, "When a ship arrived to purchase slaves, the King of Derneh sent to the chiefs of the villages in his dominions to send him a given number; but if they were not to be procured on this requisition, the King went to war till he got as many as he wanted." Captain T. Wilson, also referenced in the commission report, adds, "When they were at war they made prisoners and sold them, and when they were not at war they made no scruple of taking any of their own subjects and selling them, even whole villages at once."

Offering up criminals was another way to provide European traders with an ample supply of slaves. If a person had committed adultery, theft, or witchcraft, for instance, he or she was at risk of being sold to traders. Some individuals were even prepared to stake their liberty in gambling, and were sold if they lost.

Slave raiding parties often went deep into the African continent, up to 1,000 miles (1,600 kilometers), to get their merchandise. On such trips, it was not uncommon to lose half of the captured Africans during terrible death marches back to the slave ships. Individuals too sick or weary to keep up were often killed or simply left to die. Those who finally reached the coastal forts were herded into underground dungeons where they would remain for as long as a year, until they were boarded on ships.

Often, when slave-raiding parties would arrive at the coast only to find no ships waiting, they killed the slaves because of the expense of sending them back. Furthermore, slaves brought for sale who were rejected by the slave dealers on account of disease or otherwise were often killed because they were determined not to be worth their food.

Cruelty in the delivering of human flesh to a lifetime of enslavement knew no boundaries. As stated in the American Freedmen's Inquiry Commission report, a man named Arnold, a surgeon onboard a slave ship, or slaver, said:

> One day a woman with a child in her arms was brought to us to be sold. The captain refused to purchase her, not wishing to be plagued with a child on board. So she was taken back to shore. On the following morning she was again brought to us without the child and apparently in

great sorrow. The black trader admitted that the child had been killed in the night to accommodate the sale.

VOYAGES OF DOOM

As horrific as it was to be dragged from a village to the sea, the voyage to the New World, known as the "middle passage," was in many instances even more trying and violating. Europeans transporting slaves to markets made roughly 54,000 such expeditions. The trips often took from 60 to 90 days, but in some cases lasted up to 4 months. By the last half of the eighteenth century, more than half of all British merchant vessels were trafficking in human beings. Of the more than 30 million individuals forced into slavery in the African slave trade, about half died in Africa, with the remainder—maybe 12 million to 13 million—put aboard slave ships for the New World.

A slave's terror began the moment he or she boarded a ship and was given space for the voyage ahead to an unknown destination. "A full-grown slave takes sixteen inches in width; smaller slaves, twelve to fourteen inches," James Jones, a six-year captain of a slaver reported, as described in the American Freedmen's Inquiry Commission report. "The space they occupy when they lie on their backs is always considered sufficient for them."

As described in the PBS series *The Terrible Transformation: Africans in America*, "People were crowded together, usually forced to lie on their backs with their heads between the legs of others. This meant they often had to lie in each other's feces, urine, and, in the case of dysentery, even blood. In such cramped quarters, diseases such as smallpox and yellow fever spread like wildfire. The diseased were sometimes thrown overboard to prevent wholesale epidemics."

The scene below deck was almost unbearable. Slave rooms resembled a slaughterhouse. Slaves, by the dozens, fainted and were carried on deck. Some died there, while others were, with difficulty, restored.

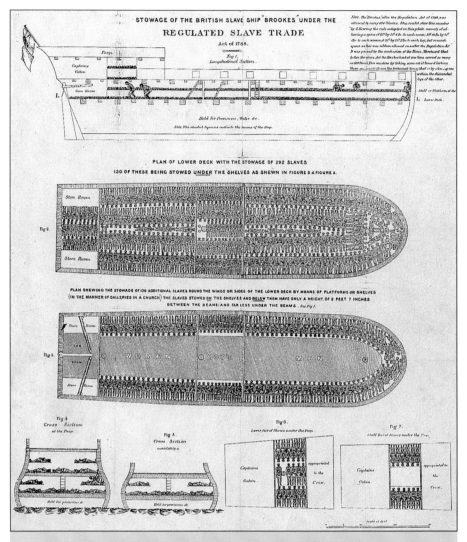

Above, *a notice to British traders illustrates the deplorable living conditions Africans were forced to endure during their transatlantic crossing.*

It is not surprising, given these conditions, that suicide was seen as a way out. Slaves would either refuse all food or attempt to jump overboard. With the former, such individuals were often severely punished for not eating, and many were found dead a day or two later. The fate of those slaves who were able to leap to a watery death may have been a blessing. As one slave who made the crossing and lived to write about it said, as quoted in *The Terrible Transformation*, "Often did I think many of the inhabitants of the deep much happier than myself."

Women and children, though not chained as the men were, nonetheless were forced into a horrifying state. Often when sitting by themselves, they could be found singing. As the American Freedmen's Inquiry Commission reported, however, the singing was " . . . always in tears. Their songs contained the history of their separation from friends and country."

Various estimates as to the slave death rate in transit are available, with 15 percent being the generally accepted figure. "About 1.8 million men, women, and children died in route, their bodies thrown overboard to the sharks that usually trailed

Slave Ship

In 1807, the British Parliament passed a bill prohibiting the slave trade, and the U.S. Congress did the same the following year. As a consequence, the naval forces of both countries patrolled the west coast of Africa, stopping suspected slave traders. When slaves were found, they were returned to Africa.

The following is an account by the Reverend Robert Walsh, who served aboard one of the ships assigned to catch such slavers. The boarding of the slave ship in question, the *Feloz*, took place on May 22, 1829.

The first object that struck us was an enormous gun, turning on a swivel, on deck—the constant appendage of a pirate; and the

the vessels," according to Marcus Rediker, author of *The Slave Ship: A Human History.*

Not surprisingly, manning a slaver was no picnic for the sailors who chose, or were forced into, such a gruesome occupation. Epidemics that were widespread among the slaves were passed to the sailors, so many a slave ship's crewmember never made a successful voyage home. There were 88 slavers that shipped out of Liverpool, England, in the years 1786 and 1787. There were 3,170 sailors aboard those ships, but only 1,428 crewmembers came back. The rest either died, deserted, or were left behind on account of illness.

A DISGRACEFUL PAGE

For the United States, the actual act of slavery began back in 1640, when three black servants living on a Virginia plantation

next were large kettles for cooking, on the bows—the usual apparatus of a slaver. . . . She had taken in, on the coast of Africa, 336 males and 226 females, making in all 562, and had been out seventeen days, during which she had thrown overboard 55. . . . As they belonged to and were shipped on account of different individuals, they were all branded like sheep with the owner's marks of different forms. These were impressed under their breasts or on their arms, and, as the mate informed me with perfect indifference, 'burnt with the red-hot iron.' Over the hatchway stood a ferocious-looking fellow with a scourge of many twisted thongs in his hand, who was the slave driver of the ship, and whenever he heard the slightest noise below, he shook it over them and seemed eager to exercise it. I was quite pleased to take this hateful badge out of his hand, and I have kept it ever since as a horrid memorial of reality, should I be disposed to forget the scene I witnessed.

Source: "Aboard a Slave Ship, 1829," EyeWitness to History, 2000.

fled the estate. They were not slaves, because slavery did not actually exist in the American British colonies at the time. Instead, they were indentured servants, bound to work for up to seven years before being released. All three were quickly caught and returned to their owner. Two had their servitude extended four years. The third, a man named John Punch, was sentenced to "serve his said master or his assigns for the time of his natural life." John Punch was made a slave—the first of what would be many, many more in the British American colonies in the years to come.

More than a century later, in 1776, the United States declared its independence from Britain. At that time, an estimated 310,000 black Africans were living in slavery within the 13 colonies. It is not well known that the majority of colonists were opposed to the institution of slavery. "The English continental colonies," according to historian George Bancroft, "were, in the aggregate [all totaled], always opposed to the African slave-trade. It was the King of England who insisted on the trade being carried out. . . . In the entire history of Great Britain there is scarcely a more disgraceful page."

In 1808, the U.S. Congress banned the slave trade itself, though not slavery per se. Yet slavery exploded, since the children of slaves were themselves slaves. The spread of slavery happened mostly, but not only, in the South, where blacks toiled nonstop on rice and cotton plantations. Tensions began to develop between Northern states, with their growing abolitionist (anti-slavery) influences, and Southern states whose survival depended directly on the "peculiar institution," as slavery was called.

In an attempt to accommodate the two regions' opposing positions on slavery, various compromises were put forth, such as the Missouri Compromise of 1820 and the Compromise of 1850. As part of the latter, the Second Fugitive Slave Act allowed Southerners to pursue runaway slaves onto Northern

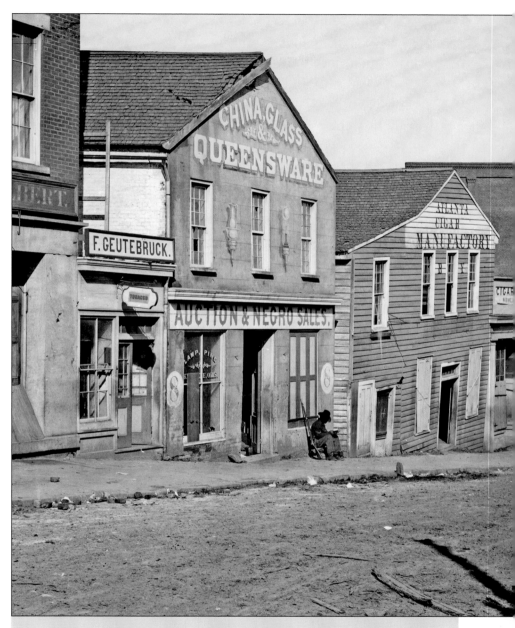

In slave auctions, men, women, and children who were up for sale were examined like horses and then placed on the auction block. Buyers would often purchase only a few slaves from an African family, resulting in many broken family trees. Above, a slave auction house in Atlanta, Georgia.

soil, and the people in the North were *required* to assist in cap-
turing and returning such slaves. The law greatly angered many
Northerners. According to Bruce Catton in *The Civil War*, "It
had an effect precisely opposite to the intent of its backers: It
aroused Northern sentiment in favor of the runaway slave."

Nothing, however, stirred anti-slavery emotions throughout the North more than the 1852 publication of *Uncle Tom's
Cabin*, written by Harriet Beecher Stowe. With sales of 300,000
in its first year, the novel told the story of a slave, Uncle Tom,
who refused to betray his fellow slaves, at the cost of his own
life. Because of the book's sympathetic portrayal of black slaves,
along with heart-wrenching descriptions of slave auctions,
thousands of Northerners rallied to the abolitionist cause.

PRELUDE TO WAR

When it came to the slave auction, the nonfiction account of
one such mass "acquiring" of slaves at a racetrack in Savannah,
Georgia, on March 3, 1859, dwarfs anything described by Harriet Beecher Stowe, at least in size. All of the slaves (chattel, as
they were called), some 439 men, women, children, and infants,
were born in the United States. The majority had never been
sold before. "Most," according to the *New York Daily Tribune* (as
reprinted in "Slave Auction, 1859," *EyeWitness to History*), "had
spent their entire lives on one of the two plantations included
in the sale."

Potential buyers had come from as far away as Alabama
and Louisiana to get what they hoped would be a good deal
for, in many cases, the purchase of entire families of a mother
and a father, along with any sons or daughters. All of Savannah's
available hotel rooms had been taken, with some buyers arriv-
ing a week or more ahead of the auction day. The slaves were
"housed" at the racetrack, put in stalls used for horses. Some
would be there for weeks, and all for at least four days before
their sale.

Slaves were brought in early so that buyers who wanted to inspect them could do so. The slaves were handled as if they were brutes, with buyers pulling their mouths open to see their teeth, and pinching their limbs to find out how muscular they were. Masters would even walk them up and down to detect any signs of lameness, having them stoop and bend in different ways to make certain there was no hidden wound.

Often, it was in the interest of the slave, particularly the male of the family, to closely watch his potential buyer and, if the buyer seemed kind, make every effort to be chosen. This would be all the better to protect his family and, above all, keep it together. The following plea of a slave named Elisha was recorded by a *Tribune* reporter at the racetrack auction:

> Look at me, Mas'r; am prime rice planter; sho' you won't find a better man den me; not a bit old yet; do mo' work den ever; do carpenter work, too, little; better buy me, Mas'r; I'se be good servant, Mas'r. Molly, too, my wife, Sa, fus rate rice hand; mos as good as me. Stan' out yer, Molly, and let the gen'lm'n see.

The begging aside, "The expression on the faces of all who stepped on the [auction] block was always the same, and told of more anguish than it is in the power of words to express," the *Tribune* informed its readers. "Blighted homes, crushed hopes and broken hearts was (sic) the sad story to be read in all the anxious faces."

The Savannah slave auction, the largest slave auction the country had ever witnessed, netted $303,850, or $6,700,000 in today's dollars. The Savannah auction may have been the biggest, yet there were many more similar auctions that caused agony for those sold again into another round of slavery. At an 1858 slave auction in Richmond, Virginia, slaves were scolded to look as cheerful and ready as possible, in order to impress potential masters. According to David W. Blight in *A Slave*

No More, "Before the slaves were exhibited for sale they were dressed and drawn out into the yard. Some were set to dancing, some to jumping, some to singing, and some to playing cards. . . . They were often set to dancing when their cheeks were wet with tears."

The market guide for the Richmond slave sale listed the average prices as follows: "For 'likely ploughboys,' ages twelve to fourteen, at $850 to $1,050, 'extra number 1 fieldgirls' at $1,300 to $1,350, and 'extra number 1 man' at $1,500." A buyer named N.M. Lee bought 95 slaves for the astounding sum of $135,785.50.

By October 1858, there were those, mostly Northern abolitionists, who had simply had enough. To them, slave auctions, indeed slavery itself, had to end—even if that meant a violent overthrow. On October 16, fiery anti-slavery orator John Brown took a handful of black and white followers and set out to seize the federal arsenal at Harpers Ferry, Virginia (now West Virginia). After taking the weapons there, they hoped to start a full-scale slave revolt in the South. His raid failed, and in December, Brown was hanged for treason.

Many in the North saw Brown as a hero who died for the cause of abolition. Those in the South had their worst fears confirmed, that the North wanted, as Bruce Catton declared, "A servile insurrection, with unlimited bloodshed and pillage, from one end of the South to the other!" The final straw came with the election of Abraham Lincoln to the presidency in 1860. On December 20, South Carolina voted to secede (withdraw) from the United States. On April 12, 1861, Southern militia bombarded Fort Sumter, a federal fort near the mouth of Charleston Harbor. The Civil War had begun.

A White Man's War

Nicholas Biddle was a 65-year-old black American from Pottsville, Pennsylvania, who was determined, from the beginning, to join the Northern cause. Biddle may have been the first to shed blood in the Civil War. On April 17, 1861, less than a week after the attack on Fort Sumter (in which, ironically, there were no deaths or serious injuries on either side), Biddle attached himself to the Washington Artillerists in response to Lincoln's call for volunteers. The unit of 530 men marched from Pottsville to Washington, D.C., and had to parade through Baltimore, a city with clear sympathy for the South. A mob of locals was quick to let the regiment know how it felt. Throwing stones, hissing, shouting, and jeering, they cried, as reported in *The Negro in the Civil War*, "Welcome to Southern graves."

Within moments, Biddle was struck in the face, "with a missile hurled by a rioter and cut so severely as to expose the bone," as declared by Edwin Redkey in *A Grand Army of Black*

Men. Cries of obscene and anti-black slurs rang in Biddle's ears. When the unit finally reached Washington, the president came out to thank the men, and it is reported that he reached over to console Biddle. Blood had been drawn in the Civil War.

The casualties would soon shock the nation, particularly the North. It would begin only two months later, at the First Battle of Bull Run. Few expected such bloodshed. Northern troops strode to the scene of battle just 40 miles (65 km) southwest of Washington, D.C., expecting a quick victory with little sacrifice.

The citizens of the nation's capital were sure that the war would be a short one and that the Union would easily triumph. Because of this, hundreds came out to see the show. They feared that if they missed the battle, there might not be another to observe. "They came in carriages, wagons, buggies, and on horseback," Bruce Catton describes in the *Civil War*. "They brought hampers of food and drink with them, and they were spread all over the slanting fields east of Bull Run, listening to the clangor of guns, watching the smoke clouds billowing up to the July sky, and in general making a holiday out of it." Soldiers, however—both Northern and Southern (but particularly the former)—would experience anything but a holiday. They would be butchered.

Lincoln had pressured the military to attack and open the way to the Confederate capital of Richmond before 90-day enlistments ended. A poorly trained Northern army of 35,000, commanded by General McDowell, reached its goal and encamped along a small stream known as Bull Run, at the town of Manassas, on the evening of July 18. The Confederates were waiting for them.

On Sunday, July 21, confusion erupted as the First Battle of Bull Run seesawed throughout the day. The Confederates blasted away, not only with guns, but also with the first use of their blood-curdling Rebel Yell. In the face of this, the Union line crumbled and retreated in disorder. Only sheer exhaustion

Nick Biddle, a former slave, was marching with the Washington Artillery through Baltimore when he was struck in the face with a brick. Famous for being the first person to shed blood during the Civil War, Biddle was not allowed to join the army because he was black. He was so well-liked by his regiment, however, that they gave him a uniform.

prevented the Confederates from chasing their enemy to its doom. It was a Southern victory and a rude awakening for the North. "We lost everything," declared William H. Johnson, as quoted in *A Grand Army of Black Men*, "life, ammunition, and honor." Johnson was one of the few black soldiers able to enlist at the time because he passed for white. He further recalled, "We were driven like so many sheep into Washington, disgraced and humiliated."

Compared to what was to come, the losses at First Bull Run were light: 2,708 for the Union and 1,981 for the Confederates. Now, however, public perceptions were changing. Would this war last a lot longer than 90 days?

BLACKS NEED NOT APPLY

It was to be a war to restore the Union, to reunite the country, and to gather back into the fold the 11 Southern states that had seceded, rebelled, and declared their independence. And, at least in the beginning, it was to be a white man's war. Free Northern blacks, 1 percent of the Union population (210,000), need not apply: Their services would not be required.

There were also close to 4 million Southern slaves at the war's outbreak. It was hardly worth discussing what contribution they might make to the Union cause. They were, needless to say, unable to directly aid the North—at least not at first.

When the war began, the U.S. government had just 16,367 officers and enlisted men in its armed services. On the day of Fort Sumter's surrender, Lincoln issued a proclamation requesting several states to raise 75,000 volunteers to put down, as declared in *The Negro in the Civil War*, "combinations too powerful to be suppressed by the ordinary course of judicial proceedings." The response was overwhelming. The whole North, East, and West were soon up in arms. Drums were beating, men were enlisting, companies were forming, and regiments were marching with banners flying.

Yet blacks were not welcome. One reason centered on the issue of time. In the beginning, many people felt the war would be over soon enough, so why get tangled up in the question of enlisting African Americans to fight? There was more to it than that, of course. There was the deep prejudice that existed throughout the North. As Benjamin Quarles declared, "That the Negro was inferior, that 'Negro blood' was different from other blood, was America's most deeply rooted misconception; and in a people's war, such as the Civil War, the prejudices of the man in the street frequently dominated the actions of elected officials and the attitude of the military."

Although African Americans were legally free in the North, they suffered from wretched discrimination. A black man could vote in only a few states (women would not gain the right until the twentieth century). A black man also could not serve on juries. In many places, he could only hold unskilled jobs or jobs in farming, and no black individual could serve in state militias—never mind that black soldiers had fought in the Revolutionary War and in the War of 1812. In 1860, however, on the eve of the Civil War, a federal law actually barred black men from serving in any land-based fighting force. There was not one African-American person in the regular army when Fort Sumter was attacked.

Some of the strongest opposition to seeing a black man in uniform came from white soldiers. "We don't want to fight side by side with the [black man]," wrote 19-year-old Corporal Felix Brannigan, as cited by Quarles. "We think we are a too superior race for that."

It was clear that in the eyes of Northern leaders and most Northern whites, this war was to be about reunification, not a fight about or against slavery. It would certainly not be a struggle that would directly engage blacks. "The North was yet a long way from inscribing upon its banners, 'Freedom for the Slave,' and it did not propose to be stampeded in that direction by the abolitionists," Quarles explained. "Rights for Negroes must be measured out in homeopathic [tiny] doses and administered with a long spoon." If you were black, the rights denied you included the right to fight for your country.

Yet African Americans would not and could not remain uncaring about the progress of the national struggle. They were determined to make a contribution and to be a part of the war effort.

WILLING AND ABLE

In spite of the restrictions before them, black men sought to enlist in the Union cause from the moment the war began. In Boston, within 36 hours after Lincoln asked for volunteers, a mammoth meeting of blacks was called at the Twelfth Baptist Church. A resolution was quickly and unanimously passed, declaring, as cited in *The Negro in the Civil War*, "Our feelings urge

Contraband Camps

Contraband camps represented freedom for former slaves, but in such camps, black families were often neglected and abused by their Union protectors. "Northern soldiers almost resented being assigned to duty guarding and policing contraband camps," according to the *Civil War Trivia Book*. "They insisted they had enlisted to save the Union, not to 'nursemaid' black refugees, and they vented their frustration on their hapless charges. In addition, the soldiers often assigned the refugees onerous [difficult] jobs that the soldiers hated to perform themselves."

Extreme hardship was often the environment in such contraband camps. The *Arkansas News* reported, as quoted on the Old State House Museum Web site, "The people who are working us to say to our countrymen that we are ready to stand by and defend the government with 'our lives, our fortunes, and our sacred honor.' "

There were those in Boston promising a force of 50,000 African-American men. "If the government would just remove the restriction placed on blacks serving in the army," a black Bostonian declared, as quoted in *The Negro in the Civil War*, "there was not a man who would not leap for his knapsack and musket and they would make it intolerably hot for old Virginia."

In New York City, a number of African Americans quietly hired a public hall and began practicing military drills, somewhat in secret, with hopes of a call to serve. In Providence, Rhode Island, a company of more than 100 blacks offered to accompany the 1st Rhode Island Regiment on its way to the front. The offer was declined briskly. Two Northern free blacks even wrote to Secretary of War Simon Cameron, pointing out that

with them [contraband] report that the blacks are encountering terrible hardships. The government is doing little for them. Much help is needed." At one camp it was reported that 25 percent of the inhabitants died within a two-year period, many from outright starvation.

Some contraband, finding conditions too difficult, even returned to slavery, as reported by eyewitness Maria R. Mann in the *Arkansas News*:

One family of 40 plantation negroes came two months since, did very well for a time, several got work, but the change of life, weather, and being robbed by our soldiers of clothing and bedding till they were greatly exposed and became sick and 13 of them died, others must die, and when their master came to persuade them to return most of them did. They did not wish to go, faltered, changed their minds daily for a week, but as destitution, persecution and death stared them in the face the sad sufferers went back.

they had voted for the administration and declared, as stated in *Forged in Battle: The Civil War Alliance of Black Soldiers and White Officers*, "The question now is will you allow us the privilege of fighting—and (if need be dying) to support those in office who are our own choice."

On April 17, 1861, a black organization called the Hannibal Guards of Pittsburgh sent a communication to General James S. Negley, militia commander of Western Pennsylvania. The message stated, as quoted in *The Negro's Civil War*, "As we sympathize with our white fellow-citizens at the present crisis . . . and as we consider ourselves American citizens . . . we therefore tender to the state the services of the Hannibal Guards." Clearly, free African Americans in the North saw the war as an opportunity to prove their worth and loyalty to the Union. At the same time, they could strike a blow at prejudice, racism, and injustice. Famed former slave and abolitionist Frederick Douglass had it right when he declared, as referenced on The American Civil War Web site, "Once let the Black man get upon his person the brass letters *U.S.* Let him get an eagle on his button and a musket on his shoulder and bullets in his pockets and there is no power on earth which can deny that he has earned the right to citizenship in the United States."

Still, the willing services of black men were refused. "This Department has no intention at present to call into the service of the government any colored soldiers," the secretary of war replied to an African American's inquiry, as described by Bruce Catton. "The Constitution will not permit me to issue an order." Blacks who rallied to Lincoln's call for volunteers faced the sad truth that, as one Northerner shamelessly announced, as cited in *A Voice of Thunder: A Black Soldiers' Civil War*, "He doesn't mean you. Niggers ain't citizens."

Curiously, the South was quick to take the black man on in its efforts to win the war, though not as a direct part of any fighting force. Southern armies soon came to depend heavily on the labor of slaves and free blacks to construct fortifications, tend cavalry horses, transport material, and perform camp services for both officers and enlisted men. Slaves on the home front raised the goods necessary to make money overseas, and labored in shipyards, armories, and ironworks to manufacture the weapons of war. It was time for the North to take notice and, if nothing else, deprive the South of such labor's advantage.

CALL ME CONTRABAND

General Benjamin Butler, a fat-faced, cross-eyed, heavy-lidded, balding "political general" from Massachusetts, had never commanded troops before. Butler was the first to see the value of ex-slaves to the Union cause. In early May 1861, Butler found himself in command of Fort Monroe, Virginia. Though he would eventually be judged a failure as a military man, Butler, a successful lawyer, did have his talents.

On the night of May 23, three runaway slaves paddled across Chesapeake Bay and up to Fort Monroe. The fugitives were given shelter for the night, and the next morning were put to work building a new bakery within the fort. Two days later, a Confederate army major named Cary, carrying a flag of truce, crossed over to the fort and met with General Butler. The following exchange took place between the two men, and would eventually lead to the most important consequences for African-American participation in the Civil War. As reported by Benjamin Quarles:

> MAJOR CARY: I am informed that three Negroes, belonging to Colonel Mallory, have escaped into your lines. I am Colonel Mallory's agent and have charge of his property. What do you intend to do with regard to these Negroes?
>
> GENERAL BUTLER: I propose to retain [keep] them.
>
> MAJOR CARY: Do you mean, then, to set aside your constitutional obligations?
>
> GENERAL BUTLER: I mean to abide by the decision of Virginia, as expressed in her ordinance of secession. I am under no

Enslaved black men and women in the South were not allowed to serve in the military, but were often forced to contribute to the Confederate war effort. Many worked in construction and nursing, while others manufactured weapons in armories or provided laundry services. Others were assigned more labor-intensive work, such as grave digging (above).

constitutional obligations to a foreign country, which Virginia now claims to be.

MAJOR CARY: But you say, we *can't* secede, and so you cannot consistently detain the Negroes.

GENERAL BUTLER: But you say you have seceded, and so you
cannot consistently claim them. I shall detain the Negroes
as contraband of war. You are using them on the batteries.
It is merely a question whether they shall be used for or
against the government. Nevertheless, although I greatly
need the labor that has providentially fallen into my hands,
if Colonel Mallory will come into the fort and take the oath
of allegiance to the United States, he shall have his Negroes,
and I will endeavor to hire them from him.

MAJOR CARY: Colonel Mallory is absent.

Calling the escaped slaves *contraband* was considered a
genius move. Butler argued that slave property, like other private property, might rightfully be taken by the army on military
grounds, as would be the case with wagons, farm implements,
wood, tools, horses, foodstuffs, cotton, and so forth. By saying this, Butler hit upon a brilliant excuse for giving refuge to
fugitive slaves. It was not emancipation; only slaves of slave-
owners in active rebellion against the Union might so be taken.
Yet the *contraband* label did offer hope to slaves who sought
such protection, while at the same time depriving the South of
a valuable resource—and gaining one for the North.

Other Northern generals soon followed up on the lead
Butler had taken. Congress, seeking a regular policy on the matter, passed the first Confiscation Act on August 6, 1861. The act
permitted the seizure of any slave being used by the Confederate military during the Civil War. Southern black slaves—not
Northern free blacks—would be the first to directly aid the
Union's military cause.

ROBERT SMALLS AND THE CAPTURE OF THE *PLANTER*

By September 1861, at least 15,000 blacks in the South had escaped "to the flag," as it was put. Former slaves everywhere were
taking advantage of the contraband policy now in place with

the majority of Union commanders. Enslaved blacks in the South sought freedom.

One such individual was a clever, and above all, patient, 24-year-old slave named Robert Smalls. He lived and worked in Charleston, South Carolina. In the processes of his daring break, Smalls not only successfully freed himself and the rest of his family, but also his brother and his brother's family. Furthermore, when Smalls delivered his party to the Union navy, he brought with him a most valuable addition: the fully loaded, high-pressure, side-wheel Confederate steamer known as the *Planter*.

On the evening of Monday, May 12, 1862, with the *Planter* docked at its wharf in Charleston Harbor, the ship's three white officers retired for the evening. Before they did so, they had given instructions to Smalls, the ship's assistant pilot, that everything be made ready for a scheduled trip the next day. Smalls, of course, accepted his directions as usual. As reported in *The Negro's Civil War*, "He did not betray his thoughts by his demeanor, and when the officers left the vessel he appeared to be in his usual respectful, attentive, efficient, and obedient state of mind. He busied himself immediately to have the fires banked, and everything put shipshape for the night, according to orders."

Soon after 8 P.M., the rest of Smalls's family, along with members of his brother John's family, boarded the *Planter*. Because the black women and children had sometimes visited the vessel, carrying food and such, nothing was suspected of their arrival by the wharf guard. Around 4 A.M., Smalls fired up the ship's boilers and cast off into the night. He moved the *Planter* slowly through the water, sounding its horn, as was the custom, careful not to arouse any suspicion of escape. Smalls was taking his time, not wanting to seem in any hurry. Because the *Planter* had often been seen moving through the harbor in the early morning hours, the guns from nearby forts, all in Confederate hands, remained silent. The ship was allowed to go about its business.

Gliding past each harbor fort, the *Planter* soon approached its last obstacle, Fort Sumter. Smalls stood in the pilot house and, according to Benjamin Quarles, "with his arms folded, after the order of Captain Relay, commander of the boat, and his head covered with the huge straw hat which Captain Relay commonly wore on such occasions, Smalls sounded the countersign with the whistle, three shrill sounds and one hissing sound." With Smalls's entire party holding its breath, the fort's watchman finally cried out, "Pass the *Planter*, flag ship for General Ripley."

The vessel continued out of the harbor, moving at a regular pace until it was beyond the range of Southern guns. The *Planter* then gained speed, lowered its Southern flags, and ran up a makeshift white flag of truce.

All was not completely safe yet, though. As the *Planter* approached the Union fleet, it faced the ship *Onward*, which was blockading Charleston Harbor. A lookout on *Onward* shouted out that a strange vessel was approaching, most likely on a ramming mission. According to Quarles, "As the *Onward's* crew stood manning the guns and on the point of sending a volley of shot, the captain caught sight of the flag of truce." The gunners relaxed. "I thought the *Planter* might be of some use to Uncle Abe," Smalls was reported to have said, as he and his "crew" transferred the ship from the Confederate States of America to the Union navy.

Smalls's actions were widely praised and reported in the North. Congress gave $1,500 in prize money to Smalls. In the months to come, the *Planter* became a most valuable asset for the Union blockade fleet in the South Atlantic.

War and Emancipation

He may not have been the man "who won the West," but he had come pretty close to it, at least in his own mind. The legendary "Pathfinder," John C. Fremont, gained a national reputation as a trailblazer of the West during the two decades before the Civil War (though it was possibly a greater reputation than he deserved). Fremont led the successful effort to wrestle California from Mexico, and he served as one of the state's first senators. In 1856, the 43-year-old explorer was chosen as the Republican Party's first presidential nominee, the youngest man yet to run for the office. Fremont had gained the party's backing in no small measure because of his strong antislavery position. Though defeated by Democrat James Buchanan, Fremont had a bold plan to demonstrate his hatred for slavery.

As a Union general, Fremont displayed little skill in military command. According to the John Charles Fremont Web site, the general "spent more energy fortifying the city of St. Louis and developing flashy guard units than equipping the troops in the field." Fremont, it seemed, faced major difficulties in coping with Rebel guerrillas who combed the countryside, destroying bridges and raiding farms at will. His forces suffered several losses, particularly a major defeat at Wilson's Creek. Clearly, if the general was to have any success, it would have to be on the political front. That was a battle he was both willing and able to pursue.

On August 30, 1861, Fremont put out an unauthorized proclamation declaring martial law throughout the state of Missouri. As part of his order, the property of secessionists, including slaves, would be taken. When the slaves were taken, however, Fremont did more than put them to work as contraband: He freed, or emancipated, them. As Benjamin Quarles observed, "The significance of Fremont's action was immediately apparent: His proclamation would shift the war's emphasis from preserving the Union to that of liberating the slaves."

Lincoln was not happy. The president wasn't yet ready to link abolition to the war effort. He felt that doing so would anger the slave-holding border states. Lincoln asked Fremont to change his order to go along with the Confiscation Act. The act, according to William Klingaman, author of *Abraham Lincoln and the Road to Emancipation*, "permitted seizure of property only if it was used 'for insurrectionary purposes.'" When Fremont refused to stick to Lincoln's request, the president had him removed from command. On September 11, Lincoln then changed the proclamation himself.

Many blacks were angered and saddened by the president's action in weakening Fremont's declaration. "The president is not now, and never was, either an abolitionist, or an anti-slavery man," said the Rev. J.P. Campbell of Trenton, New Jersey, as quoted by James McPherson. "He has no quarrel whatever with the South, upon the slavery question."

Still, there were those who, in spite of Lincoln's action, were prepared to take a more optimistic view, and to see black

Harriet Tubman was a runaway slave who repeatedly returned to the South to help guide others out of bondage. Over a period of 10 years, Tubman followed the North Star and used the Underground Railroad to bring hundreds of slaves into the North and up through Canada. She was so successful, and was such a threat to the institution of slavery, the South eventually issued a $40,000 reward for her capture.

freedom moving in a positive direction. Harriet Tubman was a former slave who helped set many of her fellow Southern slaves free. For this, Tubman became known as the "Moses" of her people. As reported in *The Negro's Civil War*, she declared, "God won't let Massa Linkum beat de South till he do de right ting. Massa Linkum he great man, and I'se poor nigger; but dis nigger can tell Massa Linkum how to save de money and de men. He do it by setting de niggers free."

On March 13, 1862, Congress passed a law forbidding the Union military to return fugitive slaves to their owners. The law applied to any slaves, be they men, women, or children. War and emancipation were indeed becoming joined.

HUNTER TAKES THE LEAD

That bind took hold in a concrete way when, in early 1862, General David Hunter, commander of the Department of the South (South Carolina, Georgia, and Florida), took two major actions: He emancipated the slaves in his territory and began to recruit them for military service.

Off the coasts of South Carolina, Georgia, and northern Florida there exists a group of islands known as the Sea Islands. When war broke out, the islands' plantation owners fled to the mainland, leaving behind thousands of slaves to fend for themselves. Union forces quickly occupied the Sea Islands, hoping to provide a haven in stormy weather for the federal blockading squadrons that patrolled the coastline. Also, it was felt that the islands would be an ideal location, given their relatively mild climate, for the training of new recruits from the North during the winter to come.

In April, Hunter and his forces took Fort Pulaski, a Confederate stronghold located near the mouth of the Savannah River. As quoted by Peter Burchard in *One Gallant Rush: Robert Gould Shaw & His Brave Black Regiment*, the general declared in May that "slavery and martial law in a free country are altogether incompatible. . . . The persons in these three states, Georgia, Florida, and South Carolina, heretofore held as slaves are therefore declared forever free."

Even though Hunter's order was quickly overturned by President Lincoln, that didn't prevent the general from taking even bolder action in the weeks to come. He recognized that his predecessor, Thomas W. Sherman, had been given authority to arm slaves if special circumstances required it. Therefore, Hunter proceeded to do just that.

In forming the 1st South Carolina Volunteers, however, Hunter gathered up freed blacks who were, in many cases, anything but "volunteers." Peter Burchard explained:

> Unfortunately, Hunter, in his recruitment of contrabands, had allowed his officers to take Negroes straight from their work in the cotton fields, giving the men no chance to say good-bye to their families and not making it clear that they would be paid and given furloughs [leaves of absence] from their regiments. This harsh tactic alienated a sizable portion of the black population and hurt recruitment in the Islands for some time to come.

In forming his regiment, Hunter had "said that he had organized no 'fugitive slaves,' but that he had, however, organized 'a fine regiment of persons whose late masters are "fugitive rebels," ' " Benjamin Quarles noted. The general was hopeful that by year's end he would have 48,000 to 50,000 men enlisted.

Lincoln at first pretended not to notice Hunter's recruiting efforts. The president eventually ordered the unit to be broken up, however, except for one company. Congress later brought back the unit. Other generals, copying Hunter, were soon busy recruiting on their own. In most cases, their recruiting efforts were done without approval from Washington.

Out in Kansas, Big Jim Lane, a U.S. senator who resigned to accept a commission as a brigadier general, began recruiting

Army Organization During the Civil War

During the Civil War, both the Union and Confederate fighting forces were organized in a similar manner, though there were differences in the number of men that made up a particular structure and what that structure was called. Both governments, the Federal and the Confederate, had Departments of War, which, in turn, were made up of armies that fought in various regions, or *theaters*. In the North, for example, there was the Army of the Potomac in the eastern theater. The South had the Army of Northern Virginia as its counterpart.

Each army, North or South, included a general headquarters, infantry, artillery, cavalry, signalmen, engineers, quartermaster, and commissary departments. From the top on down, the organization ran as follows, though there were slight differences between the North and South:

Army	16,000 men (2 or more corps)
Corps	8,000 men (2 or more divisions)
Division	4,000 men (2 or more brigades)
Brigade	2,000 men (2 or more regiments)
Regiment (cavalry)	1,200 men (12 companies)
Regiment (infantry)	1,000 men (10 companies)
Company	100 men (2 to 3 platoons)
Platoon	50 men (5 squads)
Squad	10 to 12 men

Generally, a squad was led by a sergeant or a corporal, both noncommissioned officers. A platoon would be led by a lieutenant, and a company was led by a captain. A colonel led a regiment, the most important fighting unit for the infantryman.

Source: Gettysburg National Military Park, http://www.nps.gov/archive/gett/getttour/armorg.htm.

military units of fugitive slaves from Missouri and free blacks from the North. The Department of War notified the general that he had no approval to raise a black unit. According to Joseph Glatthaar, author of *Forged in Battle*, "Lane simply ignored it in the best frontier fashion." By the time the federal government accepted the services of Lane's black regiment, its troops had already seen combat.

Clearly, the line was blurring between African-American contraband who would build forts and haul supplies and those freed slaves ready to take up arms, either to protect forts or seek out the enemy. Bit by bit, black men were enlisting to preserve the Union, and, soon enough, free their enslaved brethren.

EMANCIPATION AS A MILITARY NECESSITY

In January 1856, a Kentucky slave owner, with the aid of federal agents, cornered a group of fugitive slaves. The slaves included a mother, Margaret Garner, and her three young children—one girl and two boys. Margaret had vowed never to see her children returned to bondage. As the agents broke into the family's hiding place, Margaret quickly cut her young daughter's throat. She immediately turned to her young boys to do the same. Despite an outcry among the local population, Margaret and her surviving children were shipped down the river to the Deep South and returned to slavery. On the journey back into captivity, Margaret's youngest child died.

Such gruesome stories inflamed abolitionist feelings in the North and built the case for emancipation. A demand arose to free slaves everywhere. Yet Lincoln was still unwilling to tie the war effort to black freedom, even by the spring of 1862. The war was about preserving the Union. Emancipation, however, was clearly coming. Slowly, haltingly, but undeniably, the move was on to free the slaves.

On March 6, 1862, Lincoln sent a message to Congress asking them to pass a joint resolution offering federal money to any state that, as quoted in *The Negro's Civil War*, "may adopt gradual abolishment of slavery." With border states opposing the idea, the plan never made it through Congress. Yet black public opinion was positive and saw Lincoln's offer as a major shift in administration policy. "That the president of these United States sent a message to Congress proposing a means of securing the emancipation of the slaves, was an event which sent a thrill of joy throughout the North," the African-American newspaper the *Anglo-African* stated editorially. "It will meet with hearty response throughout Christendom."

Later in the spring, Congress abolished slavery in all the territories of the United States—and, most dramatically, on April 16, 1862, it eliminated slavery in the District of Columbia. "I trust I am not dreaming," declared Frederick Douglass, as quoted by Bruce Catton in *The Civil War*. "But events seem to be taking place like a dream."

Still, the president wavered. He declared on August 22, 1862, as stated in *The Civil War*, "My paramount [main] objective in this struggle is to save the Union, and it is not either to save or destroy slavery. If I could save the Union without freeing any slave I would do it, and if I could save it by freeing all the slaves I would do it; and if I could save it by freeing some and leaving others alone I would do that." Despite the president's reservations, the direction elsewhere was clear: Slavery would have to go, one way or another, gradually or all at once.

What finally persuaded President Lincoln to declare for widespread emancipation was not a deep desire to see slaves freed on principle. Rather, it was the need to set them free as a war necessity. The fight to restore the Union had not gone well during the 18 months since the war had begun. In battle after battle, Union forces either met defeat or failed to take advantage of Confederate weaknesses and destroy the enemy. By the summer of 1862, the Northern public, not to mention its military, was discouraged and disappointed. The war to reunite the country was dragging on and on. By the middle of July,

Lincoln had come to realize, as quoted by William Klingaman, "that it was a military necessity absolutely essential for the salvation of the Union, that we must free the slaves or be ourselves subdued."

The Union finally won a clear victory at Antietam on September 17. With the win, the president was ready to act on emancipation. On September 22, he issued what became known as his preliminary Emancipation Proclamation, declaring that on January 1, 1863, " . . . all persons held as slaves within any State or designated part of a State, the people whereof shall then be in rebellion against the United States, shall be then, thenceforward, and forever free."

DAVIS ISSUES A THREAT

President Lincoln knew that his Emancipation Proclamation, to take effect only in areas in rebellion, "would not by itself, physically deliver any slave from bondage," according to William Klingaman. Thus the president added a pledge "that no United States civilian or military official would take any action to repress such persons, or any of them, in any efforts they may make for their actual freedom."

In *The Civil War*, historian Bruce Catton summarized: "To save the Union the North had to destroy the Confederacy, and to destroy the Confederacy it had to destroy slavery. The Federal armies got the point and behaved accordingly. Slavery was doomed, not so much by any proclamation from Washington as by the necessity of war." Limited as the Emancipation Proclamation would be, its announcement in September 1862 was a giant leap forward that pushed African Americans to new levels of participation in a fight not only to restore the Union, but also to free themselves from slavery.

Many historians argue that Lincoln's issuing of the Emancipation Proclamation represented his finest hour. If this is

Frederick Douglass, one of the greatest orators in U.S. history, was a staunch abolitionist and did all that he could to end slavery. When President Abraham Lincoln issued the Emancipation Proclamation, Douglass was pleased, but also warned that negative perceptions of black people and racist social structures were not as easy to abolish as the institution of slavery.

so, one of his worst moments was his meeting with five black leaders from the District of Columbia a month earlier, on August 14, 1862. It was on this occasion that Lincoln chose to lecture his guests on the broad differences between blacks and whites, which, he felt, made it impossible for the two groups to ever live in harmony. "Whether it is right or wrong I need not discuss, but this physical difference is a great disadvantage to us both, as I think your race suffers very greatly, many of them by living among us, while ours suffers from your presence," James McPherson quotes in *The Negro's Civil War*. "There is an unwillingness on the part of our people, harsh as it may be, for you free colored people to remain with us."

The president's solution to this "problem" was to encourage blacks to leave the country and colonize parts of Africa or Latin America. Lincoln perhaps thought that colonization would make emancipation more acceptable to a prejudiced North, because freed slaves would not become part of communities in the United States. In the end, the plan gained little backing. In July 1864, Congress put an end to the idea by overturning all parts of the legislation passed in 1862 that put aside funds for colonization purposes. Still, many African-American leaders were greatly disturbed by the thought that the president even entertained such an idea.

Instead of taking up the cry to emigrate, black men were eager to take up arms. They did so in spite of a threat by Confederate president Jefferson Davis, issued on September 23, 1862, that captured black soldiers would not be treated as ordinary prisoners of war. Instead, they would be tried for insurrection (rebellion) or for causing insurrection. The penalty for such a charge was death. Under the order, black enlisted men were to "be delivered to the authorities of the state or states in which they shall be captured to be dealt with according to the present or future laws of such state or states," as cited in *The Negro's Civil War*.

Though Davis's threat was never carried out on a large scale, it did cause black men considerable concern, and rightfully so. Washington would have to assure all African Americans who enlisted that they would be protected by Union forces should they ever be captured.

JUBILEE

"Men squealed, women fainted, dogs barked, white and colored people shook hands, songs were sung," observed James McPherson in *The Negro's Civil War*. "Great processions of colored and white men marched to and fro, passed in front of the White House and congratulated President Lincoln on his proclamation. If the president would come out of his palace, he would be hugged to death." It was New Year's Day, January 1, 1863: Emancipation Day!

Jubilation was everywhere. Frederick Douglass praised the day as the most memorable in U.S. history. Yet amid the celebrations, the famed former slave and abolitionist had a serious warning for his fellow blacks, and for the nation as a whole. "The slave will yet remain in some sense a slave, long after the chains are taken from his limbs," he predicted, as quoted in *Abraham Lincoln and the Road to Emancipation*. "And the master will retain much of the pride, the arrogance, imperiousness, and conscious superiority and love of power."

Not all were quick to praise what Lincoln had done. The proclamation caused near panic in many parts of the South. The ever-present fear of slave uprisings was given new stress. Many believed the Emancipation Proclamation was an invitation for slaves to murder their masters. There was also bitter opposition in the border states. "I don't want the Negro free," declared a private from Missouri, as quoted by William Klingaman. "I don't think I will do much fighting to free the nasty thing. . . . I say the Democrats ought to go in with the South and kill all the Abolitionists of the North and that will end this war."

In the North, there was a widespread fear that blacks, fresh from the cotton fields, would flood Northern towns and cities. "The Irish and German immigrants, to say nothing of native laborers of the white race," cried James Gordon Bennett, of the *New York Herald*, "must feel enraptured at the prospect of hordes of darkies overrunning the Northern states and working for half wages, and thus ousting them from employment." Even more hostile was the warning from an opposition newspaper in Ohio, as reported by William Klingaman: "They will compete with you and bring down your wages, *you* will have to work with them, eat with them, your *wives* and *children* must associate with theirs and you and your families will be degraded to their level."

Yet despite the prejudice, fear, and paranoia displayed by many, the North as a whole gave its approval to the momentous event of emancipation. It pinned the fight to a high-sounding cause, a holy war for freedom, rather than just an attempt to restore the Union.

There was more. The Emancipation Proclamation declared "that such persons of suitable condition, will be received into the armed service of the United States to garrison forts, positions, stations, and other places, and to man vessels of all sorts in said service," as reported in *Abraham Lincoln and the Road to Emancipation*. This was the signal that African Americans had been waiting for. North and South, they rushed to join up.

The African American in Arms

At the outbreak of the Civil War there were fewer than 17,000 men in the "regular" standing Army of the United States. Since the nation's founding, most fighting units throughout the country actually had been state militias. Every able-bodied white male between the ages of 18 and 45 was responsible for military service. Most of the state units formed were called "volunteer" forces, a source of pride to the men serving. These volunteer companies selected their own officers, designed their own uniforms, drilled at their own time and place, and turned out for civic parades.

During the first year of war, Congress required the states to raise a certain number of "volunteer regiments," with service lasting from three months to three years. Soon enough, these state militia were made part of the federal fighting force. This was done mainly so their participants could be paid from the federal treasury and so such units could cross state boundaries. There were few black regiments before emancipation, and they were scattered and often unofficial. Nonetheless, the ones that were organized actually saw action.

On October 27 and 28, 1862, the Kansas Colored Volunteer Regiment fought bravely at Island Mound, Missouri, before they were even put into service, and the 1st South Carolina Colored Volunteers saw action at Township, Florida, on January 16, 1863. As quoted in *Abraham Lincoln and the Road to Emancipation*, one white observer said with admiration of the South Carolina Colored Volunteers, "Once they are in they fight like fiends. My faith is firm that the best thing that can be done for these men is to put them in the Army. They will learn there

Civil War Casualties

According to W.E. Woodward in his book *Meet General Grant*, published in 1928:

> The American Negroes are the only people in the history of the world, so far as I know, that ever became free without any effort of their own. . . . It [the Civil War] was not their business. They had not started the war nor ended it. They twanged banjos around the railroad stations, sang melodious spirituals, and believed that some Yankee would soon come along and give each of them forty acres of land and a mule.

It seems that "as far as I know" was not very far for W.E. Woodward. His claim that African Americans did not participate in fighting for their own freedom could not have been further from the truth. More than 200,000 black Americans fought during the Civil War. Of that number, 37,000 gave their lives.

Overall, about 620,000 Americans died in the Civil War. For the Union armies, in which there were between 2.5 million and 2.75 million men, the casualty estimates are as follows:

sooner than anywhere else that they are men. The improvement and bearing of those who are now in the Army is so marked that everyone notices it."

Lincoln, for one, made it his business to notice. "I see the enemy are driving at them fiercely, as to be expected," William Klingaman quoted the president. "It is important to the enemy that such a force shall *not* take shape, and grow, and thrive, in the South; and in precisely the same proportion, it is important to us that it *shall*."

Northern opinion favoring the recruitment of African Americans for combat took a decidedly new turn in the first

Battle deaths:	110,070
Disease, etc.:	250,152
Total:	360,222

Confederates numbered between 750,000 and 1.25 million. Casualty estimates for their side are as follows:

Battle deaths:	94,000
Disease, etc.:	164,000
Total:	258,000

In addition to the dead and wounded from battle and disease listed above, the Union listed:

Deaths in Prison:	24,866
Drowning:	4,944
Accidental deaths:	4,144
Murdered:	520
Suicides:	391
Sunstroke:	313
Military executions:	267
Unclassified:	14,155

Source: Burke Davis, The Civil War, Strange and Fascinating Facts. *New York: Barnes and Noble Books, 2005.*

months of 1863. It was realized then that a black man could take a bullet as easily as a white man. The reasoning was, with the war dragging ever on, and with Northern casualties ever mounting, why not let the black man fight? Indeed, the pressure mounted for him to do so as a duty. In early 1863, Chaplain George H. Hepworth wrote: "We needed that the vast tide of death should roll by our own doors," as cited by Quarles, "and sweep away our fathers and sons, before we could come to our senses and give the black man the one boon he has been asking for so long—permission to fight for our common country."

On May 22, 1863, the Department of War established the Bureau of Colored Troops to supervise and regulate the formation of enlisted black soldiers and their white officers into designated black regiments. Such units would be labeled United States Colored Troops (USCT). Eventually, more than 186,000 African-American men served as part of the USCT, and 36,000 lost their lives.

THE LOUISIANA NATIVE GUARDS

Curiously, the first black unit to be added officially into the U.S. Army was not a Northern regiment, but a Southern one. Furthermore, before taking the oath of allegiance to fight for the Union cause, the regiment had offered its services to the Confederacy. Such were the strange beginnings of the Louisiana Native Guards, an outfit that was at first commanded by black men, and the only fighting force in the Civil War ever to be so led.

Over the decades leading up to the war, New Orleans had nurtured a small but prosperous and influential population of free blacks, many of them of mixed heritage. In response to war, 1,500 such black citizens gathered to show support for Confederate Louisiana. Calling themselves "Defenders of the Native Land," they quickly formed a regiment, headed by four

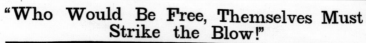

"Who Would Be Free, Themselves Must Strike the Blow!"

$200 $200

COLORED MEN
Of Burlington Co.,

Your Country calls you to the Field of Martial Glory. Providence has offered you an opportunity to vindicate the Patriotism and Manhood of your Race. Some of your brothers accepting this offer on many a well-fought field, have written their names on history's immortal page amongst the bravest of the brave.

NOW IS YOUR TIME!

Remember, that every blow you strike at the call of your Government against this accursed Slaveholders' Rebellion, you Break the Shackles from the Limbs of your Kindred and their Wives and Children.

The Board of Freeholders of Burlington Co.

Now offers to every Able-Bodied COLORED MAN who volunteers in the Service of his Country a BOUNTY of

$200 CASH! $200
WHEN SWORN INTO THE SERVICE, and
$10 PER MONTH
WHILE IN SUCH SERVICE. COME ONE! COME ALL!

GEO. SNYDER,

U. S. Steam Print, Ledger Buildings, Philada.   Recruiting Agent for Colored Volunteers of Burlington County.

After the Emancipation Proclamation went into effect, the Union began to recruit African Americans to serve in the military against the Confederate army. Many viewed it as a personal contribution for their own freedom and quickly volunteered to fight with a regiment. Above, an advertisement promises a cash incentive for African-American men who join the Union army.

black officers. When they offered their services to fight for the South, Louisiana governor Thomas D. Moore quickly accepted. Such Southern patriotism proved short lived, however. "Loyalty was to their families and home, not to the Southern cause," wrote James Hollandsworth, author of *The Louisiana Native Guards: The Black Military Experience During the Civil War*.

Indeed, when the Union navy took the Crescent City after extensive bombardment, on April 29, 1862, the Confederate Native Guards quickly disbanded, hiding their muskets and getting rid of their uniforms. As Hollandsworth noted, "The Confederate authorities never intended to use black troops for any mission of real importance. If the Native Guards were good for anything, it was for public display; free blacks fighting for Southern rights made good copy for the newspapers."

The Union capture of New Orleans found General Benjamin Butler in command. At first, the general refused to enlist black troops, but with Confederate forces still attacking, at times with considerable pressure, Butler soon changed his mind. The general called for black recruits. The response from the free black community was enthusiastic. September 27, 1862, saw the start of the first regiment of 1,000 Native Guards, now ready to fight for the Union cause. The regiment was made up not only of free blacks, but even more of contrabands who had found their way to the Union lines.

Free or former (contraband) slaves, Butler didn't care. "Better soldiers never shouldered a musket," he wrote 30 years later, as quoted in *The Louisiana Native Guards*. "They were intelligent, obedient, highly appreciative of their position, and fully maintained its dignity." Such praise aside, the general's prejudices came through when he chose to add, "They learned to handle arms and to march more rapidly than most intelligent white men, because from childhood up, the word of command had been implicitly and abjectly obeyed by the Negro. His master's voice was his perfect guide."

Black recruits poured in. By November, Butler had put together two more regiments, the 2nd and 3rd Native Guards. These new regiments were made up almost entirely of former slaves, not free blacks. The regiments were now officially members of the Union army, and Butler dressed his black soldiers in the finest blue available, parading them down Canal Street on a bright Saturday afternoon in late fall. The white people of New Orleans, it was reported, stared with disgust.

PORT HUDSON AND THE PROOF IS THERE

John Crowder was only eight years old when he went to work as a cabin boy on the Mississippi River. Earning a mere five dollars a month, he turned it all over to his mother, whose husband had abandoned the family shortly after the boy's birth in 1846. After four years on the river, John had worked his way up to steward, the highest position a black man could hope to achieve on a river steamboat. In the process, he had taught himself to read and write.

When General Butler began raising his black regiments, Crowder sought to join, hoping to serve the Union cause and earn a steady income to send home. The 16-year-old Crowder hid his age and not only gained admission into the 1st Louisiana Native Guard, but did so as a lieutenant. He thus became one of only four black officers to serve in a fighting Union force, and probably was its youngest member—black or white.

Andre Cailloux did not need to hide a thing in order to gain an officer rank with the 1st Louisiana Native Guard. Educated in Paris and speaking both English and French, Cailloux was a natural leader in the New Orleans black community. He was a splendid horseman and an excellent athlete. Furthermore, unlike many of the black elite in the Crescent City, Cailloux had no European blood. He was proud to be, as he often declared, "the blackest man in New Orleans."

In April of 1862, Cailloux volunteered to fight for the North. He personally recruited a company (100 men) for the 1st Louisiana Native Guard. As captain, he was said to be firm and just, as he whipped his men into shape, barking orders in English and French for all to understand.

One of the main goals of Union forces in the third year of the war was to wrestle control of the Mississippi River from the Confederates, and thus split the South in two. In May 1863, Port Hudson (100 miles, or 160 km, north of New Orleans and very much in Confederate hands) stood in the way of that Union goal. General Nathaniel Banks, who had replaced General Butler as commander in New Orleans, was ordered to head north out of the Crescent City and take Port Hudson on the Mississippi River. It would be no easy task. The Confederates, some 6,000 strong, had put up a threatening defense. Of particular concern to Union forces was the wide, swampy area leading up to the garrison's high bluffs. Storming those bluffs would prove to be an extremely difficult undertaking.

On the evening of May 26, Crowder, Cailloux, and the 1,080 men making up a pair of black regiments of the Native Guard waited in readiness to attack at dawn. They were told that black soldiers were to lead the army's charge. This was the chance for the African-American soldiers to prove their bravery, their moment of truth.

It was a disaster in planning. As the black regiments got within 200 yards (180 meters) of the main Confederate works, the enemy "opened with a hail of canister shell and rifle fire that ripped through the lines of black troops," as reported by Joseph Glatthaar. "By dint of sheer determination, the men pressed onward to their slaughter."

Both Crowder and Cailloux fell early in the engagement. The Confederates refused to allow Union soldiers to retrieve the "niggers," and so both men's lifeless bodies were left to rot for weeks. "Had an officer with authority and any sense examined the Confederate position, the charge of the 1st and 3rd Louisiana Native Guards would never have taken place," declared Joseph Glatthaar. " . . . it should never have happened."

It was not until July 1863 that Port Hudson surrendered. Though the May 26 attack was a failure, word flew from the Mississippi Valley of the brave deeds and valor of the black soldiers who fought. The battle at Port Hudson marked a turning point in the nation's attitudes toward black soldiers. "My Co.

was apparently brave," reported a lieutenant in the 3rd Louisiana Native Guard, as cited in *Freedom's Soldiers*. "They fought with great desperation and carried all before them. They had to be restrained for fear they would get too far in unsupported. They have shown that they can and will fight well."

RECRUITING THE OFFICERS

African-American soldiers were trying to prove their courage at every turn, but were they being held to an unfair, higher standard? "If the men of a colored regiment should fail, as for various reasons many white regiments had done," Peter Burchard observed, "their failure would be attributed to their race."

To minimize any such defeat, it was decided early on that United States Colored Troop regiments would be officered by white men only. African-American soldiers would be recruited, trained, and led into battle not by men of their own color, but by whites. Officer commissions would be reserved for white men of distinction and proven leadership qualities. The whites' only excuse for this restriction rested on a number of weak assumptions. The Lincoln administration believed it could ease the nervousness of many white Northerners by making it clear that black units would be officered only by whites. It would let Americans know that whites would always be in charge.

Feeding on that prejudice was the added belief that blacks, once they were in a position to fight their former masters, would go on wild killing sprees. White officers were assumed to be disciplined and assured, and would therefore be able to hold black soldiers in check—or so it was claimed.

Furthermore, there was the simple issue of patronage. Commissions were highly sought after in the Civil War, as in all previous wars. Giving them to influential whites was a way to gain support for the cause at hand. Even so, it soon became clear that the government had every intention of selecting truly

During the Civil War, white officers led black regiments in an attempt to deflect negative sentiments against African Americans if these units were defeated in battle. Organized in 1861, the 1st Louisiana Native Guard (above) was a militia of free black men that fought at Port Hudson, Louisiana, against the Confederacy. Their bravery and determination helped the Union understand the strength and potential of black regiments.

capable men for USCT leadership. To become an officer in a United States Colored Troop regiment was a highly selective process. For the most part, it was a process based on qualifications and merit.

Previous military experience was a requirement for any-one seeking to lead black troops, but that alone would not suffice. "I am desirous to have of its officers young men of military experience, of firm anti-slavery principles, ambitious, superior to a vulgar contempt for color, and having faith in the capacity of colored men for military service," Massachusetts governor John A. Andrew wrote when seeking to form a black state regiment, as reported by Joseph Glatthaar. "Such officers must necessarily be gentlemen of the highest tone and honor."

To achieve that goal, a tough examination and interview process awaited any applicant who sought a USCT commission. "Anyone if he has money can get a position in a white reg't but not so here," wrote Henry Crydenwise, once he received his USCT commission, as reported in *Forged in Battle*. "[Here are] a better class of men, more moral, more religious, better educated and they understand their business better than those in white reg'ts." Crydenwise guessed that more than one-half the officers in white regiments could not have passed the examination he had taken.

Indeed, there were practical, down-to-earth reasons for wanting to be an officer, in either a black or a white regiment. Officers could resign at any time, a luxury that did not exist for enlisted men. In addition, officers received much better pay, and, of course, there was the prestige associated with rank. As Glatthaar put it simply, "Officers had their privileges." Still, it was clear from the start that USCT white officers wanted to make a difference. They wanted to strive to make black units equal to or better than white organizations. Only time would tell whether they would be able to do so.

FILLING THE RANKS

Enticing blacks into the ranks of the USCT proved to be a challenge. In many cases African-American men needed little push to take up arms: With the offer of freedom to any man who enlisted, plus the opportunity to fight to free his brethren, many Southern blacks risked their lives to make it from bondage to the Union lines. "I travels all that day and night up the river and follows the North Star," one escaping slave remembered, as reported in *Forged in Battle*. Hiding during the day, moving by night, and eating nuts, berries, fish, and rabbits, the slave nearly starved to death during his trek north. "One day, he heard guns firing in the distance, but he could not tell whether Union or Confederate troops were in front of him," Joseph Glatthaar continued the narrative. "Tired, hungry, and scared, he did not know what to do, when suddenly some soldiers sneaked up on him and ordered him to raise his hands. Fortunately, they were Federals, and he was soon within Union lines, clad in a blue uniform."

For many blacks, however, a recruitment effort was necessary to bring them into the Union army. Civilian recruiters were hired to scour the land in an effort to bring black men into the service. The recruiters often were corrupt, thinking only of making money, and were living hand-to-mouth as they searched out potential recruits. All the time, they were dodging Confederate guerrillas. Such recruiters contributed little to overall African-American enlistments. By the end of the war, they had registered fewer than 5,000 black soldiers.

As it turned out, the burden of black recruitment was left mainly to USCT officers, much to their annoyance. In the South, where blacks had been Union contraband, such officers or potential officers had mixed success. Black men were all around, and, in many cases, convincing them to go from camp laborers to putting on blue uniforms was not difficult. On the other hand, had such contraband been given better treatment, they might have been quicker to trust recruiters who often promised what could not be delivered. At times, getting an escaped slave to sign up was a tough sell.

Not so with blacks in the North, however. With African-American leaders such as Fredrick Douglass in full support, blacks flocked to recruiting offices. In the end, more than 34,000 African Americans of the North served in the Union army. This was more than 15 percent of the entire free black population of 210,000 in 1860.

In preparing their men for combat, USCT officers worked to, above all, teach discipline to their enlistees, and it was only through drilling exercises that such discipline could be taught. Drilling was the learning of different battlefield formations and maneuvers. These exercises were key to the units' success. "I knew that nothing but drill, discipline, and more drill, would fit the regiment for the field in such condition as to give every officer and soldier absolute confidence in the ability of the regiment to take care of itself under any and all circumstances," declared a colonel, as quoted in *Forged in Battle*.

Some thought that black soldiers had a natural ability to drill. It was claimed that their love of music and dance would prepare them well for combat structure. Yet a more likely reason for their accomplishments was that black soldiers "pay better attention and take more pride in it than white soldiers do," as one lieutenant said, as quoted in *Forged in Battle*.

Success in drill preparation was all well and good. For African-American soldiers, however, as with whites, the true test of their training came only in combat. This was something in which they were eager, even desperate, to take part.

The
Massachusetts 54th

It was a splendid spring day in Boston, May 28, 1863, the perfect weather for a grand parade. City authorities were anticipating trouble, however; and they were ready. A large party of police had been assembled under Chief Colonel Kurtz. Unknown to the public, larger reserves of patrolmen were held out of sight, all in readiness should rioting break out. At least 20 blacks had chosen to arm themselves, and as the Massachusetts 54th Regiment of African-American troops gathered into a marching stance, they were comforted knowing they had been given six rounds of ball cartridges, just in case. "The unit's rear guard marched with fixed bayonets," reported Donald Yacovone in *A Voice of Thunder*.

The city need not have worried. All turned to joy and celebration as the North's first black regiment took to promenading down Beacon Street before shipping out for duty in South Carolina. Thousands of well-wishers had poured into Boston by train, coming to view black soldiers in blue: parading and marching, disciplined and confident. Shouting broke out everywhere. "All along the route, the sidewalks, windows, and balconies were thronged with spectators, and the appearance of the regiment caused repeated cheers and waving of flags and handkerchiefs," Peter Burchard reported. "Merchants suspended business for the day to join the men and women, black and white, who filled the streets and the windows of countless flag-draped buildings along the parade route," echoed Donald Yacovone.

Leading the Massachusetts 54th was just the kind of man whom Governor John Andrew had spoken of when he called for white officers of distinction, devoid of prejudice, and prepared to make a difference. Robert Gould Shaw was, indeed, an inspired choice. Born in Boston to a well-known abolitionist family, Shaw was just 25 years old when the state's governor handpicked him to command the 54th.

Upon the outbreak of war, Shaw had quickly sought military service. He was with the 7th New York Infantry Regiment that marched to the defense of Washington, D.C., in April 1861. A month later, with his initial 30-day enlistment over, Shaw joined the 2nd Massachusetts Infantry as a second lieutenant. The young Shaw remained with the 2nd for the next two years and saw action, most notably at the Battle of Antietam, after which he was promoted to captain. Shaw had demonstrated his resolve in combat, had attended Harvard University, and had voiced strong opposition to slavery. As such, Shaw was an obvious pick when abolitionist leaders went looking for a white officer to lead black troops.

Yet Shaw had his doubts, not so much about African Americans as a fighting force, but rather in his own ability to lead such a group. After all, should an officer choose to command a black regiment, other people would not necessarily accept or approve of his choice. "In this new negro-solider venture, loneliness was certain, ridicule inevitable, failure possible,"

Civil War Small Arms

At the outbreak of the Civil War, both sides were forced to use out-of-date and mismatched weaponry. Eventually, however, standard issue rifles and firearms became available. Below is a brief discussion of weapons available to the infantry and cavalry.

Infantry

The basic weapon for the infantryman, particularly in the North, was the single-shot, muzzle-loading percussion musket known as the Springfield. The Springfield had a barrel 39 inches (1 m) long that could fire a .58-caliber bullet at a target 500 yards (460 m) away. Production of this musket reached 1.5 million by the war's end.

A close cousin to the Springfield was the British-made Enfield. More than 800,000 of them were sold to both the North and South during the war. The Enfield had a .577-caliber bore and, like the Springfield, was capable of hitting a target of up to 500 yards with reasonable accuracy. The Enfield was a good enough weapon, but some of its parts were hand-finished. The Springfield, on the other hand, was all machine-made. Thus, with the Enfield, different parts were not always able to fit perfectly into different weapons.

Cavalry

The main shoulder weapon for cavalry soldiers during the Civil War was the short-barreled carbine, effective at 200 yards. According Bertram Barnett of the Gettysburg National Military Park, "They [the carbines] ranged from fairly simple single-shot breechloaders using a paper or linen cartridge and a percussion cap, to complex repeaters firing self-priming metallic cartridges. Calibers ranged from .44 to .54, and many carbines took specially made cartridges. Resupply of ammunition often proved tedious."

wrote William James, as quoted in *One Gallant Rush*. "Shaw was only twenty-five, and although he had stood among the bullets at Cedar Mountain and Antietam, he had till then been walking on the sunny side of life."

Nonetheless, Shaw eventually said yes to a black-regiment command. Now, in late May 1863, after months preparing his troops for service, he had taken his place upon a white horse to march his soldiers down to the waterfront. Ships stood by to take the regiment southward, to what the men hoped would be a chance to prove their valor. "I was not quite 18 when the regiment sailed," remembered Ellen Shaw, Colonel Shaw's sister, as recalled by Peter Burchard. "My mother, Rob's wife, my sisters and I were on the balcony to see the regiment go by, and when Rob riding at its head, looked up and kissed his sword, his face was as the face of an angel and I felt perfectly sure he would never come back."

BAPTISM BY FIRE

The 54th arrived in the South prepared for battle and ready for a fight. They dreaded their own army's reluctance to place them on the front lines far more than the Confederate troops whom they would fight. Despite Island Mound and Port Hudson, and with their traditional role as laborers a given, they still had a lot to prove. Shaw feared that higher-ups would be all too willing to force blacks to exchange their rifles for picks and shovels—or if not that, they would be assigned to guerrilla warfare, a form of combat that would bring them no honor. The 54th would see its share of fatigue duty (cleaning, digging, draining, and the like), and there would be days of boredom spent swatting mosquitoes, dodging alligators, and jostling with snakes. There would be plenty of action soon enough, however.

On June 4, Shaw's regiment put up a simple, temporary camp on a plantation outside the town of Beaufort, on Port Royal Island. It was a wondrous place, particularly for soldiers

African Americans who enlisted in the Union army had to prove themselves to Northern whites who did not believe they were up to the task. In 1863, the New York Tribune stated, "Loyal Whites have generally become willing that [black soldiers] should fight, but the great majority have no faith that they will really do so. Many hope they will prove cowards and sneaks—others greatly fear it." The Louisiana Native Guards, also known as the Corps d'Afrique (above), became an example of the bravery and determination of black soldiers during the fight at Port Hudson, Louisiana.

who had come from the temperate North. "The South Carolina Sea Islands, caressed by bright sunny skies, are blessed with warm, sandy soil, luxuriant evergreens, towering cypress trees, and expansive oaks draped with sweeping moss," Donald Yacovone wrote in *A Voice of Thunder*. "Fig, palm, and orange trees, oleander as high as a house, and enchanting lilies with stems as thick as a man's thumb graced some of the most re-splendent plantations of the South." Remaining at Beaufort for only a few days, the regiment was soon ordered to board troop transports for a raid on Darien, Georgia. It would not be the 54th's finest hour.

By the time the regiment arrived at Darien, the town was virtually deserted. Still, Colonel James Montgomery, the regi-ment's brigade commander, ordered the 54th and other units to sack the town. Shaw protested, but with no success. He tried to keep his men in line, but the availability of so much loot was just too tempting. "The men came back to the square on their way to the wharves like overloaded peddlers, carrying furniture and other personal belongings," wrote Peter Burchard. "Cows were led through the streets by lengths of rope and torn sheets."

Darien proved an embarrassment for the entire 54th. Shaw feared, rightly so, that a campaign of plunder and robbery would hurt the reputation of black troops everywhere. It would take valor on the battlefield to erase what had happened at Darien, and Shaw was now desperate to avenge the regiment's honor.

The 54th got its chance soon enough. On July 11, the men were ordered to James Island, a Confederate stronghold that the South was determined to hold. Four days later, Shaw sent three of his companies (about 300 men) out on picket duty, expecting a Confederate attack. The attack indeed came, with 900 Reb-els yelling shrilly as they swarmed down on the 54th's picket line. Union soldiers faced a barrage of canister and gunfire. "The bullets fairly rained around us," recalled black sergeant R.J. Simmons in a letter to the *New York Times*. "When I got there the poor fellows were falling down around me, with piti-ful groans."

In their fighting, however, the three companies of the 54th were able to help the retreat and escape of the 10th Con-necticut, a white regiment that had been trapped in a cul-de-sac. "They fought like heroes," one of the Connecticut troops wrote, as quoted by Joseph Glatthaar. "But for the bravery of three companies of the Massachusetts Fifty-fourth (colored), our whole regiment would have been captured." The embarrassment of Darien had been forgotten.

IMPENETRABLE FORT

Charleston, South Carolina, is where it had all begun. It was where Southern secession was born. Nestled in a protective bay, the city had remained stubbornly in Confederate hands since the war's outbreak, when Rebel soldiers took Fort Sumter, centrally located at the mouth of Charleston Harbor. In 1863, in addition to Sumter, the harbor was guarded by other island forts: Fort Moultrie, Fort Johnson, Battery Gregg, and, most threatening, Fort (Battery) Wagner, near the tip of Morris Island. Union forces desperately wanted Charleston, but to get it the navy would have to run straight through the middle of the group of Confederate forts, the strongest of which, by far, was Wagner. To take Charleston, the Union would first have to capture Fort Wagner.

Wagner was considered an engineering marvel. It was constructed of compact sand and palmetto logs, said to be the strongest earthwork ever built. Its parapets and traverses were thick and high, while a ditch in front of the fort made it even more difficult to invade. The battery, where ammunition and powder were stored, boasted a roomy bombproof shelter capable of protecting nearly 800 men when enemy fire became hot.

Not only was Fort Wagner well built, but it was also cleverly designed. Two corners of the fort projected outward, which enabled the defenders to fire on attackers from the front and side at the same time. For added safety, the Confederates had prepared a moat 3 feet (1 m) deep just outside the first wall and a rifle pit located 200 yards (180 m) beyond that.

It was Wagner's strategic location, as much as its earthwork fortress construction, that gave the fort its tough reputation. "Its position was formidable," Peter Burchard describes in

One Gallant Rush. "It stretched from the Atlantic on the east to the marshes of deep, meandering Vincent's Creek on the west and could only be approached by direct assault along a spit of sand, narrow even at low tide." At high tide, the situation for would-be attackers was depressing. There lay a strip of land only 25 feet (8 m) wide, a critical factor that Union planners had overlooked.

Apart from that strip of land, Union forces were otherwise well aware of what they faced as they prepared to seize Fort Wagner. On July 10, a flotilla of Union troops from nearby Folly Island crossed Lighthouse Inlet, on the southern edge of Morris Island. They landed and quickly built counterbatteries. Within days, 41 pieces of artillery were placed at distances of 1,300 to 1,900 yards (1,200 to 1,700 m) south of the fort. It was hoped that in cooperation with guns from the Federals' fleet in the waters off the northern tip of Morris Island, "it might be possible to tranquilize Wagner's armaments, demoralize her defenders, and thus mount a successful attack," as Benjamin Quarles put it.

On the morning of July 18, the "softening up" operation began. "Nothing like the rapid discharge from heavy artillery had ever been seen or heard before on this continent," wrote the *Richmond Examiner*. "The air was filled with a bursting volley of iron as the shells struck Wagner's slope and bounded over her parapet."

Having thrown no fewer than 9,000 solid shot and shell at Wagner in an 11-hour period, the Union command believed it had done what was needed. According to Benjamin Quarles, "The enemy's armament had been irreparably damaged and the defenders of the garrison were disabled or demoralized." Nothing, however, could have been further from the truth. The Confederates suffered only 18 casualties, and their guns and ammunition were safely secured in bombproof sand pits. The Union forces were now readying themselves for Confederate attack. The Massachusetts 54th, in particular, was in for a rude surprise.

SHOCK TROOPS AND CANNON FODDER

The action at James Island had cost the 54th 14 dead and 30 wounded or missing, but the regiment's conduct had impressed General George Crockett Strong, the Union field commander. He promised Colonel Shaw that in the future, he would place the 54th "where the most severe work was to be done and the highest honor to be won," as quoted in *A Voice of Thunder*. To that end, the black regiment was given a day of rest. It was then ordered out on what would be a terrible two-day march across James Island and Morris Island to Fort Wagner. Historian George W. Williams described the scene in *The Negro's Civil War*:

> All day they marched over the island under the exhausting heat of a July sun in Carolina, with the uncertain sand slipping under their weary tread. All night the march was continued through darkness and rain, amid thunder and lightning, over swollen streams, broken dikes, and feeble, shuddering, narrow causeways. . . . This dreary, weary, and exhausting march was continued till six o'clock in the morning of the 18th, when the Fifty-fourth reached Morris Island. . . .

By nightfall, the exhausted, hungry, and thirsty regiment had taken its place at what would be the lead assault column. Shaw, standing at the head of his formation, called on his men to prove themselves. As the regiment waited in the dimming light for word to attack, enemy cannonballs fell and then rolled at their feet. "I guess [they kind of expect] we're comin," one man joked, as recorded in *A Voice of Thunder*.

A half-hour later, the regiment rose to the charge "at the double quick." The bugle sounded. "Over the half mile of Morris Island sand the storming blacks led the way, with their colonel in the vanguard [front]," reported Benjamin Quarles. "No

The storming of Fort Wagner (above) resulted in devastating losses for the celebrated Massachusetts 54th Regiment, one of the first African-American units in the Union army. Led by Robert Gould Shaw, the soldiers were ordered to attack Fort Wagner, a fortification in South Carolina. Although some were able to reach the stronghold's outer walls, Union troops were eventually forced to retreat.

sentinel [watchman] hoarsely cried out in challenge; from Wagner came not a shot."

Then madness broke out. Wagner lit up like a volcano, spewing shot and shell over the advancing charge. The regiment staggered under the shock, the wounded screaming and falling all about. Those who survived, having somehow forged the fort's moat, had now to gain the parapet, to climb up the sloping sides of Fort Wagner. "But the Rebel fire grew hotter on our right, and a field piece every few seconds seemed to sweep along our rapidly thinning ranks," a black sergeant later wrote, as referenced in *The Negro's Civil War*. "Men all around me would fall and roll down the scarp into the ditch."

Shaw and some of his men reached the top of the parapet. The colonel was seen there waving his sword and shouting to his troops, "Rally! Rally!" An instant later, a bullet pierced Shaw's heart, and he fell forward into the fort. "I saw his face," a survivor was quoted as saying, in *The Negro's Civil War*. "It was white as snow, but in every line was the courage which led his men to the very crest of that wall of death."

The retreat that followed turned into a mad panic. "Union soldiers shot their own men, others surrendered, and a few slid down the embankment to make their way to safety through hissing bullets and bursting shells," reported Donald Yacovone. "When they reached Union lines, the horrified men found the rear guard drunk and shooting retreating soldiers, particularly blacks."

GLORY AND PAIN

It would take weeks to finally determine how many men were lost at the battle to take Fort Wagner (which later was determined to be virtually impossible to take). When the casualty count was complete, the results were horrifying and had never before been experienced. Of the estimated 1,700 Confederates defending the fort, only 174 were killed. Union forces, on the other hand, lost 1,515. There had been 10 Federal regiments that took part in the assault. The Massachusetts 54th was the hardest hit. It had thrown 600 men and 23 officers into the fight, and 247 were killed, wounded, or captured—more men than the entire Confederate casualty total.

The casualties and the assault itself were unnecessary. The failure of white brigades to support the first attack left the 54th stranded. Had help come when it should have, the outcome might have been different. Strategically, Fort Wagner, and

Charleston itself, might not have been much of a prize. "The department's major military operations, the seizure of Wagner, the invasion of Florida, and the siege of Charleston, proved disastrous and pointless."

Under a flag of truce, Union commanders searched for Colonel Shaw's body. According to an account by John T. Luck, a captured Northerner, Confederate commander Johnson Hagood told him, "I knew Colonel Shaw before the war, and then esteemed him," as quoted in *The Negro in the Civil War*. "Had he been in command of white troops, I should have given him an honorable burial; as it is, I shall burry him in the common trench with the Negroes that fell with him."

When Shaw's father learned of his son's fate, he was reported to have said, "We hold that a soldier's most appropriate burial-place is on the field where he has fallen," as quoted in *Forged in Battle*.

The 54th's assault on Fort Wagner had been a failure. Black soldiers, however, had proved themselves to the North. It is clear enough that if the Massachusetts 54th had faltered, 200,000 colored troops might never have been put into the field. Instead, the 54th had made Fort Wagner a name to remember for decades to come. "Wagner was a turning point in the war," Benjamin Quarles noted. "The valor of 600 enlisted men of the Fifty-fourth opened the floodgates for the fresh army of more than 180,000 Negro soldiers who would infuse new spirit into a war-weary North. The brave black regiment thus blazed a path which would wind its way to Appomattox."

Northern Bigotry

"A" is for Abolitionist, "B" is for Brother, "C" is for Cotton-field, and "D" is for Driver. So it went in *The Anti-Slavery Alphabet*, published in 1847. The preface to the alphabet book, as cited in *Children for the Union: The War Spirit on the Northern Home Front*, informed little readers that although they were young, they could still contribute to the anti-slavery cause:

> *Even you can plead with men*
> *That they buy not slaves again . . . .*
> *Sometimes, when from school you walk,*
> *You can with your playmates talk,*
> *Tell them of the slave child's fate,*
> *Motherless and desolate.*

Blacks made up a tiny minority of the Northern population at the Civil War's outbreak. African-American populations in cities such as New York and Boston were not more than 2 percent. Even so, their cause—emancipation—was the fire that had brought the nation to war. From their first victory, with Congress's abolition of the slave trade in 1808, to Lincoln's Emancipation Proclamation of 1863, abolitionists had been fighting an ever-expanding battle to see the nation free from slavery.

The North sought to end slavery on moral grounds. Many Northerners, however, had strong racist beliefs about African Americans. Many felt that it was one thing to see the black man free, and it was quite another to give him political, economic, and social equality with whites.

The reason for these feelings was that many people believed that blacks, as a people, were biologically inferior to whites. So-called "race scientists" of the nineteenth century had pushed a basic idea that slaves were biologically subhuman, and therefore, so were blacks. They called their studies on racial differences "niggerology," in the words of Louis Agassiz, a Harvard zoology professor. These beliefs were typical of Northern bigotry. When black waiters served Agassiz in a hotel dining room one evening, he complained in a letter to his mother, as quoted in *Complicity*, "Seeing their black faces with their fat lips and their grimacing teeth, the wool on their heads, their bent knees, their elongated hands, their large, curved fingernails, and above all the livid color of their palms, I could not turn my eyes from their faces in order to tell them to keep their distance."

Indeed, the Supreme Court's *Dred Scott* decision of 1857 made clear the African American's economic, social, and political problems. The court's decision famously declared that blacks were "altogether unfit to associate with the white race, and had no rights which the white man was bound to respect," as quoted in *The Long Pursuit: Abraham Lincoln's Thirty-Year Struggle with Stephen Douglas for the Heart and Soul of America*.

Even Lincoln himself had been less than a champion of liberal thought. In 1858, he said in a debate with Stephen

"We'll Hang Jeff Davis on a Sour Apple Tree"

In an attempt to rally Northern support for the war, encouragements of patriotism began in the schools, even in the lower grades. Some children wrote and acted in war plays, inspired by the conflicts in the North and South. A boy named Charles Skinner took the lead in directing such productions, as described in *Children for the Union*:

> A wide variety of characters, from soldiers and sailors to planters and slaves, "formed the characters in Charlie's tragedies which were given in our cellar kitchen," where the young entertainer had chalked scenes on the walls. "Properties were few and poor, but our imaginations were rich": a packing case became a cell called a Libby Prison, "a board tilted on a sawhorse" became Seminary Ridge, empty barrels became cotton presses, and washtubs turned into gunboats.

Such patriotism aside, on the schoolyard, as in real life, there was a lack of agreement about whether the war should continue, and for what purpose. "Disagreements" that adults expressed—with Republicans generally for the war and Democrats opposed—spilled over onto the school playground. According to *Children for the Union*:

> A Baltimore orphanage was seized by a "warlike spirit" that brought bickering and wrestling to every recess, while a Minnesotan remembered with relish the power that lay behind such epithets as "Rebel," "Copperhead," and "black Republican," as well as the "certainty of being able at any minute to stir up a fight simply by marching up and down aggressively" and singing that favorite wartime anthem of children, "We'll Hang Jeff Davis on a Sour Apple Tree."

Students, by their actions in school and out, reflected tensions in the adult North over the need to fight for reunion and emancipation.

Douglas, as cited in *The Long Pursuit*, "I am not nor ever have been in favor of bringing about in any way, the social and political equality of the white and black races. I am not, nor ever have been in favor of making voters of the Negroes, or jurors, or qualifying them to hold office, or having them marry with white people."

Still, as the war to reunify the country and free the slaves struggled on in the summer of 1863, it was becoming clear to many Northerners that the black man could, would, and should do his part in fighting for the cause. Furthermore, with the military draft now a reality, it became obvious that not only could a black man take a bullet—he also could take a place. In a bow to equality, African-American men would, by the spring of 1864, become just as subject to the military draft as white men.

RICH MAN'S WAR, POOR MAN'S FIGHT

Conscription is the forced enrollment of people for military service. It is never popular. When the Union resorted to such a measure in March 1863, it was a clear sign that the war for them was not going well. A year earlier, however, in April 1862, the South had put in place a similar action, with similar anger from its citizens. Only a year after the war's outbreak, the Confederacy had been forced to conscript white men between the ages of 18 and 35. It made an exception only for planters who held public office or owned 20 or more slaves. Yet the knowledge throughout the North that the South, too, was suffering from manpower shortages did little to relieve anxiety and opposition to the Northern draft. "All who wish to be butchered will please step forward," suggested one newspaper editorial, as quoted in *Abraham Lincoln and the Road to Emancipation*. "All others will please stay at home and defy Old Abe."

Northerners were particularly concerned that the draft would subject them to a three-year term of service, if not for the full duration of the war—however long that would be. Being

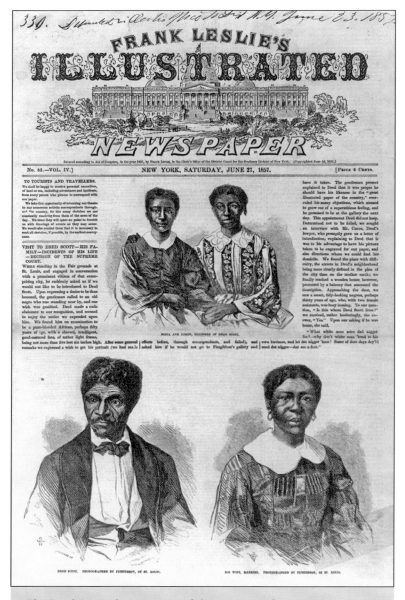

The Dred Scott *decision, one of the most significant Supreme Court rulings in U.S. history, was a public affirmation of the racist attitudes of many white people toward blacks. In the case, the slave Dred Scott petitioned for his freedom. Supreme Court justices based their judgment on the fact that, as a slave, Scott was not considered human but mere property. Above, an issue of* Frank Leslie's Illustrated Newspaper *features an article on Dred Scott and his family during the court case.*

required to enlist for 30 days (as was the case when enthusiastic men rushed to join at the war's outbreak) was one thing. Three years—clearly a full-time, long-term commitment, to say the least—was another.

To gain recruits, the North, from the beginning, had "requested" volunteers from the various states. It was the responsibility of each state to meet a given quota. If they could do so with volunteers, all was well and good. If not, a state would have to resort to various forms of bribes or rewards to attract eligible men. The most widespread one was a bounty system in which the governing body would pay someone to enlist. The bounty scheme wound up costing the various state governments a fortune and, by most accounts, did far more harm than good.

It was not uncommon for a man to receive more than a thousand dollars for joining the army. With that kind of money to be had, it was no surprise that the poor of society would show up to take the money. Often, the dishonest recruits did so more than once. Known as "bounty jumpers," such men, according to Bruce Catton, "had no intention of rendering any service at the front and would enlist, collect their bounty, desert at the first opportunity, reenlist under another name in some other locality, collect another bounty, desert again, and go on with the process indefinitely. . . . Not one in eight of the high-bounty recruits ever did any useful service at the front."

What really upset Northerners, however, were certain ways that one could avoid service, exceptions that were truly only available to the wealthy. If one were called by the draft, he might, if he could afford to, hire a substitute to take his place. "Any drafted person furnishing an acceptable substitute," said the *New York Times*, "is exempt from military service for the period for which said substitute is mustered into the service."

Furthermore, if one could raise $300 to be paid to the federal treasury, he could also be excused. In such a case, however, a man would still be subject to future drafts, should they be necessary. Either way, finding a substitute or paying the fee (the latter supposedly there to encourage one to find a substitute rather than collect money for the government) led to the obvious observation that this was a "rich man's war and a poor man's fight." Under such a system there was bound to be frustration and anger, leading to explosion. That explosion was not long in coming.

FULL-BLOWN RIOT

It was called Five Points: the intersection of five streets in the Sixth Ward, near what is today Columbus Park in lower Manhattan. In the mid 1850s, it was hell on earth. English novelist Charles Dickens, an expert on urban poverty and decay, called the area "worse than anything he had written about in *Oliver Twist.*" As James McCague quoted in his book *The Second Rebellion: The New York City Draft Riots of 1863*, Dickens reportedly called it "a place of murder and robbery and all that is loathsome, drooping, and decayed is here." Five Points was home to the "lowest of the low," the Irish immigrants, and it was also where the majority of free New York blacks lived.

In a book titled *Hot Corn*, an anonymous American writer echoed Dickens, when he described Five Points' slum buildings, called tenements. The author declared, as quoted in *The Second Rebellion*, "Here is a Negro and his wife sitting upon the floor . . . eating their supper off the bottom of a pail." Often when people died in Five Points, they were buried on the spot. "In one such den, a little girl stabbed to death for the penny she had begged, lay unnoticed for nearly a week before her mother finally scraped a shallow grave in the dirt floor and disposed of the corpse."

By July 1863, the city's local draft boards were ready to call their first conscripted men, mostly from the lower classes, and in particular the slum dwellers of Five Points. By this time, it was not surprising that a powder keg of anger had risen. On

July 13, 1863, a protest mob's rage was best expressed when its leader Charles Chapin declared, as cited in *The Second Rebellion*, "There would have been no draft but for the war—there would have been no war but for slavery—the slaves were black—*ergo*, all blacks were responsible."

What had started out as a mass protest to stop the draft fanned quickly into a full-blown, three-day race riot, where thousands were killed or injured. It is the worst such disaster in U.S. history.

Up to 15,000 rioters swarmed the city, burning and pillaging in protest, battling police and soldiers from rooftops and intersections. Meanwhile, New York's helpless black population bore the main force of the violence. James McPherson reports in *The Negro's Civil War*:

> Having been taught by the leaders of the Democratic Party to hate the negro, and having but a few weeks previously seen regiments of colored volunteers pass through New York on their way south, an infuriated band of drunken men, women, and children paid special visits to all localities inhabited by the blacks, and murdered all they could lay their hands on, without regard to age or sex. . . . Hundreds of the blacks, driven from their homes, and hunted and chased through the streets, presented themselves at the doors of jails, prisons, and police-stations, and begged admission.

The Colored Orphan Asylum was sacked and burned. Its 200 children, none of them more than 12 years old, barely escaped with their lives through a back door.

As New York City burned, the Massachusetts 54th Regiment, 500 miles (800 km) to the south, prepared for battle with Confederates at Fort Wagner. More than a few African-American soldiers who would soon die trying to take the Southern fort had, unknown to them at the time, family members killed or injured in a Northern catastrophe that would tarnish a city for decades to come.

A SOLDIER'S DUTY AND A SOLDIER'S PAY

Black soldiers pressed on, despite racist attitudes in the North, at least those of Southern sympathizers. These soldiers displayed courage at every turn and in every battle, and strength and fortitude in the face of clear acts of discrimination within the army itself. Some of the worst suffering came in the form of unequal pay. This not only forced unbearable hardship on African-American soldiers and their families, but also, at times, threatened to destroy their willingness to serve.

When black male contraband were recruited to serve in the Union forces, they were paid a laborer's wage: $10 per month. When they began to serve as soldiers, it was determined that their pay should remain the same, *minus* a $3 clothing allowance. In reality, they received just $7 per month. By contrast, white soldiers were given $13 per month *plus* a clothing allowance. Thus the highest-ranking black man was paid only slightly more than half of what the lowest-ranking white soldier received. Noncommissioned black officers, such as sergeants and corporals, if they had been white, could have received between $17 and $21 per month. Instead, they were still paid only $7. This happened in spite of the fact that, at least early on, blacks were promised that they would be paid at the same level as their white counterparts.

The hardship and injustice of the pay difference was angering and hurtful and was allowed to go on for far too long. "Our debasement is complete," wrote a soldier from the Massachusetts 55th (an all-black regiment recruited on the heels of the 54th), as quoted in *A Voice of Thunder*. "No chance for promotion, no money for our families, and we [are] little better than an armed band of laborers with rusty muskets and bright spades." Trouble was inevitable. "Few people ever

The Union refused to pay its African-American troops a wage equal to their white counterparts. This angered many people, including a corporal who wrote to President Lincoln saying, "We have done a soldier's duty. Why can't we have a soldier's pay?"

realized how close the black troops came to full mutiny," wrote Donald Yacovone. "A broken promise on equal pay made blacks doubt that justice would be forthcoming on all other issues."

On November 19, 1863, William Walker, an African-American sergeant of the 3rd South Carolina Volunteers (21st USCT), decided he had had enough. Walker marched his company to his captain's tent and ordered them to stack arms, thus refusing to perform any service until equal pay was approved. On February 29, 1864, Walker was court-martialed and shot for mutiny.

The Walker case attracted enormous attention throughout the North. Massachusetts governor John Andrew provided a most fitting tribute to Sergeant Walker. He wrote, as cited in *Forged in Battle*, "The government which found no law to pay him except as a nondescript or a contraband, nevertheless found law enough to shoot him as a soldier."

By mid-June of 1864, Congress finally allowed full and equal pay to black soldiers. The promise of pay would be good for any back pay as far back as January 1, 1864, *if* the black soldier had been free on April 19, 1861. Thus, under the act, only blacks who were already free before the war were eligible for equal pay. To get around this obvious insult, Colonel Edward N. Hallowell, commander of the Massachusetts 54th, made up a "Quaker Oath," a pledge none of his men could refuse. They and other black soldiers throughout the Union agreed, as quoted by Joseph Glatthaar, that "You do solemnly swear that you owed no man unrequited labor on or before the 19th day of April, 1861, so help you God." When they stated this, the issue of equal pay was finally put to rest. Though it was a scheme meant to get around Congress's ruling, the oath let all blacks claim, rightly so in their eyes, that slavery was a sham and that they had never rightfully belonged to anyone.

COMMISSIONS DENIED

Of course, pay was not the only issue that angered black soldiers. There was also the denial of officer commissions to blacks. This related controversy would take longer to resolve, with a far less satisfactory outcome.

As possibly the most important black correspondent of the Civil War, George Stephens had an upfront position with African-American troops as they took their place on the front lines of conflict. These days, the term *embedded* is used to describe news reporters who go out with the soldiers on whom they report. Long before today's modern embedded journalists, Stephens was embedded with the Massachusetts 54th. Stephens exposed himself to the same hazards in combat as enlisted men, but he was not an enlistee. He was a commissioned officer of sorts, though not one in the chain of command. Such black men, few as they were, were granted commissions only as chaplains or surgeons.

When the soldiers of the 54th stormed Fort Wagner, Stephens was with them. When the black soldiers retreated in disarray and their own Union comrades fired on them, Stephens took a bullet that temporally paralyzed his right hand. After its crushing defeat, the 54th's Union commanders immediately put the tired regiment to work digging trenches in front of Wagner. Stephens did not complain at first, though he was to write later, according to Donald Yacovone, "The Fifty-fourth has become a group of 'ditchers, not soldiers,' the spade and shovel is their only implement of warfare."

Many of the 54th's commissioned officers were killed or wounded at Wagner. Noncommissioned officers such as Stephens, therefore, found themselves unofficially commanding their companies, taking the place of commissioned officers in formation. Such black men hoped that they might finally be given the commissions they felt they had earned since they had shown such bravery in battle. As soon as possible, Stephens and others in the same position were busted back into the ranks.

The Confederate evacuation of Fort Wagner on the early morning of September 7, 1863, provided some relief for the war-weary 54th. Still, the regiment's men were greatly bothered for years to come that their more distinguished noncommissioned officers did not advance in rank.

In the end, it was determined that the refusal to appoint qualified African-American soldiers to officer rank throughout the Union army was blatant discrimination—nothing more. Major General Banks replaced General Butler in New Orleans, and substituted black officers with white ones, citing embarrassment and demoralization as his reasons.

The federal government finally gave in and chose, ever so carefully and infrequently, to appoint black commissioned officers at the close of the war. Indeed, when it did so, many white officers were furious. Then in January 1865, Colonel Hallowell recommended Stephens for promotion, and his request was denied. Governor Andrew of Massachusetts approved of the commission but it was turned down because of Stephens's race.

Yet, in the end, Stephens received a sort of payback. The 54th returned to Boston on September 2, 1865, to a welcome that rivaled its famous departure two years earlier. Despite the Department of War's ruling, Stephens assumed the position of first lieutenant, and, as quoted in *A Voice of Thunder*, "with his men marched triumphantly over Beacon Hill where Boston's black community turned out en masse to greet them."

Freedom's Siren Call

There was a land of Cavaliers and Cotton Fields called the Old South. Here in this pretty world, Gallantry took its last bow. Here was the last ever to be seen of Knights and their Ladies fair, of Master and Slave. Look for it only in books, for it is no more than a dream remembered, a civilization gone with the wind . . .

So opened the 1939 film *Gone With the Wind*. It was based on the hugely successful novel of the same title that had been published three years earlier and written by Margaret Mitchell. The author's work sought to show a pre-war, pre-industrial "Old South" that celebrated gentlemanliness and honor. Hers was a society built on a planter class, where a few rich and pampered elite supported themselves with the labor of a contented, even happy, African-American slave underclass. Although the former was true, the latter was anything but.

Nonetheless, in order to justify going to war for what J.B. Calvert declared "the worst cause that men ever fought for," white Southerners had to see their support of slavery in the most gentle, even helpful terms. "I am almost ready to acknowl-edge that the African is happier in bondage than free," a South-ern master was reported to have said, as quoted in Charles Jonyer's *Down by the Riverside: A Carolina Slave Community*. "At least one thing is certain: nearly all of the free negroes I have seen in the North were miserable creatures—poor, ragged, and often criminal. Here [in the South] they are well-clad, moral, nearly all religious, and the temptations that demoralize the free blacks in our Northern cites are unknown to, and cannot, approach them."

Of course, in reality, such a family-friendly society as the plantation supposedly encouraged was far less happy and peace-ful from the slave's perspective. As Jonyer continues, "Families don't tie up their loved ones and whip them mercilessly. Fami-lies don't rape their own young daughters. Families don't pub-licly hang their kin. Families, therefore, were not plantations, but were rather inhumane excuses for agricultural profit that shaped the Southern black experience forever."

With the start of the Civil War, the plantation-based eco-nomic and social structure came crashing down. Quick to fall was the belief among some planters that their slaves would re-main faithful, in spite of the temptations of freedom—not so. "I have seen the favorite and most petted negroes the first to leave in every instance," said a slave owner's wife, Ella Clanton Thomas, as quoted in *A Slave No More*. "Those who we loved best, and who loved us best—as we thought, were the first to leave us."

The war progressed and Union armies moved deeper into the South. It soon became clear that slaves would seek ref-uge and escape to freedom no matter what, given any chance. "Wherever Union armies moved, they were followed by long lines of fugitive slaves," Bruce Catton declared. "Unlettered folk who did not know what the war was about and could not imag-ine what the future held, but who dimly sensed that the road trodden by the men in blue was the road to freedom."

Long before the war started, however, most Southern planters were well aware of the desire of their slaves to seek liberty. Masters had always experienced unacceptably high

Mixing Races

By one estimate, 250,000 mixed-race persons existed in the United States during the time of the Civil War, and they were almost always the product of a union between a white male slave-owner and a black female slave. When held in bondage, it was often assumed that a biracial person, particularly a female, was better treated than a black slave. Being a master's child and of relatively light skin, perhaps such a person, even in slavery, would be given a better life than his or her full-black brethren. As Frederick Douglass reported in his *Narrative of the Life of Frederick Douglass, an American Slave*, the opposite was more often the case:

> ... it is worth to remark that such slaves invariably suffer greater hardships, and have more to contend with, than others. They are, in the first place, a constant offence to their mistress. She is ever disposed to find fault with them; they can seldom do anything to please her; she is never better pleased than when she sees them under the lash, especially when she suspects her husband of showing to his mulatto [biracial] children favors which he withholds from his black slaves. The master is frequently compelled to sell this class of his slaves, out of deference to the feelings of his white wife; and, cruel as the deed may strike any one to be, for a man to sell his own children to human flesh-mongers, it is often the dictate of humanity for him to do so; for unless he does this, he must not only whip them himself, but must stand by and see one white son tie up his brother, of a few shades darker complexion than himself, and ply the gory lash to his naked back; and if he lisps one word of disapproval, it is set down to his parental partiality, and only makes a bad matter worse, both for himself and the slave whom he would protect and defend.

numbers of male slave runaways. They were therefore forced early on to increase the number of black females, in spite of their dimmer economic worth. This was intended to stabilize the African-American slave population. It was hoped that married male slaves with children would be less likely to try and escape. It worked only up to a point. Freedom proved to be a siren call that could not be muffled, no matter what dangers and uncertainties it involved.

ESCAPE ROUTES

"Agents" or "shepherds" were those who helped slaves find the "railroad." "Conductors" were those who guided slaves along the route. "Stations" were hiding places beside escape paths. "Stationmasters" hid slaves in their homes or barns. The escaped slave was known as a "passenger" or a "cargo," and one who aided the "railroad" financially was known as a "stockholder."

These were the code words used to identify parts of one of the most celebrated slave escape mechanisms created, the so-called Underground Railroad. Though it was rarely actually under the earth, the Underground Railroad was "underground" in the sense that it was a secret undertaking to provide a route for slaves of the South to escape to the North.

It is estimated that between 1810 and 1850, thousands of slaves escaped via the Underground Railroad's secret pathways and safe houses. Individuals who participated in the undertaking were rarely told more than they needed to know about the overall operation. In order to maintain secrecy, a single person or small group knew only of their particular link in the overall scheme. Thus a conductor might pass a passenger on after taking the slave, most often by night, 10 to 20 miles (16 to 32 km) down the line. Stationmasters provided food and rest for the escaping slave during the daytime, sending him or her forth at night to complete the next link

One of the many ways black men and women could escape bondage was through the Underground Railroad, a network of like-minded citizens who were willing to help runaway slaves (above). Southern slaves traveling to the North were often told to look for simple indications of a welcoming home, like a lone lantern hanging on a porch of someone's house. The trek toward freedom ended in Canada, a destination that could take anywhere from two months to a year to reach on foot.

in a harrowing journey, where capture was an ever-present possibility.

The most celebrated of all Underground Railroad conductors was a former slave named Harriet Tubman. During a 10-year period, Tubman was known to have made 19 trips, entering deep into Southern territory to escort more than 300 slaves to freedom.

In 1849, Tubman began with her own escape. Fearing she would be sold, the 29-year-old set out from her Maryland plantation at night, following only the North Star. She eventually made it to Philadelphia, where she found work and saved her money. Then, the following year, she returned to Maryland to escort her sister and her sister's two children to freedom. Soon after, she made a second trip to Maryland to rescue her brother and two other men. On a third journey, Tubman sought her husband, only to find he had married another woman. Not wanting to return empty-handed, Tubman brought back other slaves seeking freedom. Soon enough, the feisty, stubborn, and resourceful Tubman found that she had become a conductor extraordinaire on the Underground Railroad.

Again and again Tubman returned to the South to rescue slaves wanting to escape to the North. According to *Judgment Day*:

> Tubman devised clever techniques that helped make her "forays" successful, including using the master's horse and buggy for the first leg of the journey; leaving on a Saturday night, since runaway notices couldn't be placed in newspapers until Monday morning; turning about and heading south if she encountered possible slave hunters; and carrying a drug to use on a baby if its crying might put the fugitives in danger.

Tubman even packed a gun on her rescue trips, but not to fend off slave seekers. Rather, it was to threaten her fugitive charges if they weakened in their determination to carry on. "You'll be free or die," she told them.

She was called the Moses of her people. Frederick Douglass said of her, as quoted in *Judgment Day*, "Excepting John Brown—of sacred memory—I know of no one who has willingly encountered more perils and hardships to serve our enslaved people than Harriet Tubman." John Brown, himself, agreed. He declared that Tubman was "one of the bravest persons on this continent."

WALLACE TURNAGE, COUNTRY SLAVE

Wallace Turnage, born a slave in 1846, attempted his first escape from an Alabama plantation in 1860. He was only 14 years old. Having been beaten numerous times in the span of less than a month, Wallace was determined to run away. Yet soon enough, the young man's first attempt at seeking freedom failed when he was overcome by hunger and forced to return to his plantation.

Even though Wallace knew he would be severely punished for his escape attempt, the muscular youth was determined not to bow to his overseer's whip. When the whip came, Wallace fought a two-hour wrestling brawl with his white attacker, a man named Horton. In an autobiography Wallace later penned, he claimed to have gotten the best of Horton in the fight itself. With the help of other slaves, however, Horton finally was able to tie Wallace to a tree. The price of resistance was 95 lashes, all given to Wallace with an evil delight by the angry overseer.

Within a year, Wallace was off again. This time, the 15-year-old was able to cross the state line into Mississippi, about 27 miles (43 km) from where he had left, in Pickensville, Alabama. "Encountering a white man with a shotgun," David Blight wrote in *A Slave No More*, "bullets flew by his 'ears and shoulders cutting the leaves like so many hornets,' but he outran them." Unfortunately, the now "wild and half-starved" Wallace blindly circled back toward Pickensville. His second escape attempt ended like the first one, on the plantation he had fled.

On his third try at seeking freedom, Wallace made it much farther and stayed away a great deal longer than on either of his previous two attempts. Yet this undertaking, too, would end in disaster. "Heading north toward Tupelo, Mississippi, where he could at least hope to eventually reach the Union armies, Wallace struggled against bloodhounds, the winter cold, near starvation, and extreme brutality until he was finally captured," wrote historian David Blight. "[He] was destined to be caught by the police state of slavery in wartime Mississippi."

This time Wallace received a severe beating that almost took his life. "Captured, interrogated, and tortured by white men who did not believe that he could hail from so far away, Wallace was pistol-whipped and stabbed through his thick coat," David Blight wrote. "One of his sadistic interrogators smashed his head repeatedly into the bricks under the mantel of a fireplace and threw the slave into the fire as though to kill him. . . . The burned and bloodied youth was taken by handcar down the railroad back to Alabama."

Wallace might have taken advantage of what the Underground Railroad had to offer, but the fiery and combative youth often preferred to go it alone. After laboring from February to August 1862 on a plantation owned by James Chalmers, Wallace made a fourth attempt at escape. It led to failure once more. This time Wallace had made a beeline for the Union army he knew was concentrated around Corinth, Mississippi. Again, Wallace, not yet 17, was captured. He spent two months held in the house of the Confederate bounty hunter who had caught him. Eventually, his owner, Chalmers, came to retrieve him.

Not surprisingly, Chalmers quickly took Wallace to the city of Mobile and sold him. The teenager was now an urban slave, where he was soon to discover that seeking freedom would be, if not easy, a bit less difficult. Liberty finally came to Wallace, when, on his fifth attempt at escape, he was able to literally row himself across the Mobile Bay waters to Yankee-held Fort Powell. "I now dreaded the gun and handcuffs no more," Wallace eventually wrote in his autobiography, reprinted in *A Slave No More*. "I could now speak my opinion to men of all grades and colors, and [have] no one to question my right to speak."

JOHN WASHINGTON, CITY SLAVE

John Washington's route to freedom was a lot different than the one taken by Wallace Turnage. Washington was a light-skinned man of mixed race, born on May 20, 1838, in Fredericksburg, Virginia. In the end, he would literally walk away from bondage.

In his first autobiography, *Narrative of the Life of Frederick Douglass, an American Slave*, Douglass wrote that "a city slave is almost a free man, compared with a slave on a plantation." In that sense, Washington, who spent his teenage years in bondage in an urban environment, was "blessed" with freedom of movement, along with an opportunity to earn an income. These were advantages Turnage never could have imagined. Washington was quick to seek the benefits.

For reasons not entirely clear, Washington's mother, Sarah, was able to learn to read at an early age. She passed on the gift of literacy to her son, forcing him to spend up to two hours per day at his lessons. By the age of 10, "John was as equipped as his struggling mother could make him in the insecure world of slavery," wrote David Blight in *A Slave No More*. "Washington could read; he had learned to wear pants; he was honing his negotiation skills with his mistress and other white people." And in 1848, he was living in the city where, as David Blight continues, "the boundaries of slavery were permeable [able to be crossed]."

Over the next decade, Washington became a trusted slave employed by various masters. With that trust, owners were willing to give the now young man the ultimate advantage he would need to seek his freedom. Between 1859 and 1862, Washington was "hired out" several times.

Though only 25,000 of the 246,000 enslaved Virginians in 1860 were hired out, a master enjoyed obvious benefits in doing so. "The common practice of slave hiring only verified the

In an attempt to weaken the Confederacy by taking away their free work force, President Abraham Lincoln declared that fugitive slaves (above) behind Union lines were considered to be property, and therefore "contraband of war." This classification encouraged slaves in the South to leave their masters to join Union forces, where they provided labor for construction and domestic services.

average slaveholder's primary goal 'to get as much out of them [slaves], and expend as little on them, as possible," David Blight reported. "Each worker was given a designated goal for his labor (his owner was paid for his time); beyond that expectation the slaves were paid extra money for any higher production, allowing the worker in some weeks to garner four to five dollars for himself, a significant sum in 1860." Washington, as a hired hand, was putting such dollars in his pocket, all the better to prepare himself for his day of escape.

On January 3, 1862, Washington married a free black woman named Annie Gordon. Washington was now 24 years old and he had literacy, a wife, some freedom to do as he pleased, and money stashed away. In other words, he had all the motivation in the world to make a dash for freedom. His opportunity came on April 18, 1862—almost exactly one year after the Civil War began. As Union and Confederate armies collided outside of Fredericksburg, John Washington seized the moment. Working at the Shakespeare Hotel as a trusted aide, he was given a roll of banknotes to pay off all the servants. Washington was then ordered to close up the hotel and take the keys to a safe place.

After handing out the payroll and ordering drinks for everyone, Washington sped down to the Rappahannock River. Union watchmen stationed on the opposite bank waved to him, motioning for him to cross. Washington took a small rowboat and, with a partner, he paddled across the river to freedom, where he would eventually rejoin his wife.

SEA ISLAND EXPERIMENT

Unlike Turnage and Washington, the slaves occupying the Sea Islands off the South Carolina coast did not have to plan elaborate escapes—individually or in groups—when the war began. Freedom came to them in one fell swoop, when the Union navy secured the islands in November 1861. There were about 10,000 abandoned slaves there. At first they received little comfort from Union commanders, who generally let the slaves fend for themselves. By January of the following year, many were seriously ill or actually starving.

Union forces became more and more concerned by the realization that they were sitting atop the largest cotton crop in recent memory. They wanted that cotton harvested as quickly as possible, so it could be shipped to the North as a valuable trade good. Who would do it, though, and what type of motivation would be required to get them to pick it?

"Will the people of African descent work for a living?" Treasury Department official Edward Pierce asked rhetorically, as quoted in *Abraham Lincoln and the Road to Emancipation*. When Pierce completed his initial report to the department on February 3, 1863, he was optimistic. "The Negroes on the islands already had begun to awaken from the deadening impact of slavery," he enthused. Thus began a most interesting experiment to see if blacks would work to secure cotton without being forced to do so, if they would harvest a crop for a wage. There would be much more to it than that, however.

The Sea Islands were destined to become a proving ground for freedom, one that attracted masses of Northern abolitionists, both men and women. They came not only to supervise the planting of cotton on a free-labor basis, but also to teach the ex-slaves to read and write. They attempted to uplift them, to prove to the world that former slaves could be educated, trained, and prepared for freedom. The most famous of these idealistic reform groups was known as Gideon's Band.

The experiment itself was concentrated on the island of Port Royal, and became known as the Port Royal Experiment, or a "rehearsal for reconstruction," according to Eric Foner, author of *Reconstruction*. Central to the trial was the desire to educate ex-slaves and, above all, to teach them to read. "There is one sin that slavery committed against me which I will never forgive," an ex-slave declared, as Donald Yacovone reported in *A Voice of Thunder*. "It robbed me of my education."

Indeed, before the war, in places like Virginia and South Carolina, a black child could be whipped if he or she were found getting any schooling at all. That did not stop Suzie King Taylor, a slave born in 1848. Taylor was brought up by her grandmother in Savannah, Georgia. "My brother and I being the two eldest, we were sent to a friend of my grandmother, Mrs. Woodhouse, a widow, to learn to read and write," Taylor reported in her 1902 autobiography, *A Black Woman's Civil War Memoirs*. "We went every day about nine o'clock, with our books wrapped in paper to prevent the police or white persons from seeing them. . . . After school we left the same way we entered, one by one, when we would go to a square, about a block from the school and wait for each other."

Taylor was among the ex-slaves in Port Royal in 1862. Here, along with the Gideonites and other Northern missionaries, she tried to pass on her knowledge and her unquenchable desire to learn to interested ex-slaves around her. The African-American hunger for education stemmed not only from the pure desire to learn, but also from the belief that the schoolhouse would be the first proof of independence. It would be the beginning on the road to full participation in a new nation being reborn before one's eyes.

African Americans Stake Their Claim

In early 1864, as the Civil War entered its fourth year, there seemed no end to the suffering experienced by both the North and the South. The Union, with 533,000 men in arms, commanded the largest army the world had ever seen. Yet the Confederacy fought on, determined to wear down the North to a point where public opinion would throw up its arms and let the South go its own way.

In that belief, however, the South was in denial. The North would continue to press forward, determined to defend positions taken, defeat Southern armies, and gain and hold additional territory. At Fort Pillow in particular, 40 miles (65 km) north of Memphis, Union forces were determined to defend the strategic fort on top of a hill along the Mississippi River.

Early April 1864 found Fort Pillow protected by 577 troops—285 of them white, 292 black. On April 12, a Confederate force of 1,500 under the leadership of General Nathan Bedford Forrest arrived, bent on taking the federal fort. After a fierce day of murderous bombardment, Forrest demanded the complete, unconditional surrender of Fort Pillow, which was under the overall command of Major William Bradford. When Bradford refused, Forrest ordered his bugler to sound the charge.

In the battle that followed, Union forces suffered severely before finally surrendering when it was clear there was no possibility of relief. The Union experienced terrible losses during the fight, and so what happened immediately after the surrender raised a controversy that to this day still has not been completely resolved. In what became known as the Fort Pillow Massacre, some two-thirds of all black soldiers at the fort lost their lives. By contrast, Confederates killed 36 percent of all white troops. "An undetermined number of Union soldiers, mostly Negroes, were murdered in cold blood after they had surrendered," wrote historian James McPherson in *The Negro's Civil War*. "A Congressional committee charged that at 'least 300' of the Union troops were massacred."

In the investigation that followed the battle, 21 African-American survivors of Fort Pillow were questioned. As quoted in *The Negro's Civil War*, Sergeant Benjamin Robinson's testimony was particularly moving:

> QUESTION: Were you at Fort Pillow in the fight there?
> ANSWER: Yes, sir.
> QUESTION: What did you see there?
> ANSWER: I saw them shoot two white men right by the side of me after they had laid their guns down. They shot a black man clear over into the river. . . . They told me to lie down, and I laid down, and they stripped everything off me.
> QUESTION: This was the day of the fight?
> ANSWER: Yes, sir.
> QUESTION: Go on. Did they shoot you?
> ANSWER: Yes, sir. After they stripped me and took my money away from me and they dragged me up the hill a little piece, and laid me down flat on my stomach. . . . I got up and commenced crawling down the hill; I could not walk.

Led by General Nathan Bedford Forrest, the future founder of the Ku Klux Klan, Confederate forces killed many black Union soldiers at the Battle of Fort Pillow in Tennessee (above). The majority of white Union soldiers survived, while only 62 members of the black troops survived the fight. Accusations that the Confederates had gone too far led to a Congressional investigation and continued controversy over what has come to be known as the Fort Pillow Massacre.

QUESTION: When were you shot?
ANSWER: About 3 o'clock.
QUESTION: Before they stripped you?

ANSWER: Yes, sir. They shot me before they said, "come up."

QUESTION: After you had surrendered?

ANSWER: Yes sir; they shot pretty nearly all of them after they surrendered. . . .

Fort Pillow was clearly a case where Southern forces wanted to show Northerners that no mercy would be given to black soldiers. They would be treated not as prisoners of war, but rather as fugitive slaves. For African-American soldiers, the response was, "Remember Fort Pillow." In the coming months, they vowed to fight on. The murdered black soldiers at Fort Pillow, it was promised, would be avenged.

THE BATTLE OF THE CRATER

In mid-June, General Ulysses S. Grant, now commander of all Union forces, decided on a surprise attack on Petersburg, a critical Confederate railroad center 22 miles (35 km) south of Richmond. Grant sent in the 18th Corps, made up of three divisions. One division contained a black brigade, which was in turn made up of four infantry regiments, two of cavalry, and two of batteries.

There were 3,000 African-American soldiers who fought bravely in the first Union assault on June 15 on the railroad town. Nonetheless, their losses were high. The 4th U.S. Colored Troops alone lost 250 men out of fewer than 600. Still, the bravery the black soldiers showed had impressed their white counterparts. "No nobler effort has been put forth today, and no greater success achieved than that of the colored troops," said their commander, General "Baldy" Smith, as quoted in *The Negro in the Civil War*. "They have displayed all the qualities of good soldiers."

Still, Petersburg held. The Union army would now have to lay siege to the town. Federal forces were encamped about 500 feet (150 m) from Rebel-held lines, and could gaze up on a fort that stuck out over the Confederate station. If that fort could somehow be reduced, an assault on Petersburg itself might succeed.

The Union troops were made up of a number of regiments. One, the 48th Pennsylvania Infantry, was made up of former coal miners. "They came up with the idea of digging a tunnel under the enemy lines, planting gunpowder at the end of it, and blowing up the enemy fort," according to the *Civil War Trivia Book*. "Army engineers declared their plan impossible since they would have to dig a tunnel 500 feet (150 m) long, and no mine had ever been dug so far." Nonetheless, the 48th dug. It took them five weeks, but in the end they were able to plant 8,000 pounds (3,600 kilograms) of gunpowder in 320 kegs under the unsuspecting Confederates.

On June 30, 1864, the Union mine was blown up, blasting a crater nearly 200 feet long, 60 feet wide, and 30 feet deep (60 m long, 18 m wide, and 9 m deep). "No one present ever forgot the spectacle," wrote Benjamin Quarles. "The shock was like that of an earthquake, accompanied by a dull, muffled roar. Then came the incredible sight of men, guns, and caissons being vomited two hundred feet in the air."

Unfortunately, in what would from then on be known as the Battle of the Crater, Union forces had literally dug their own grave. Black troops were originally chosen to lead the battle charge, but, according to Joseph Glatthaar, "for fear of political repercussions if the endeavor failed and black troops sustained huge losses, Major General George Meade had a white division head the attack." Then Glatthaar continues, "As a result of mismanagement, Confederate obstinacy, and the difficulty of crossing the huge crater, the white troops soon stalled and the Federals sent in the black division to exploit the break in the Confederate line."

A major disaster followed. Confederates fired on the confused and trapped white and black Union soldiers from both the front and sides. "Most Federals, rather than surrender and risk their fate with their enemies fell back in perfect disorder, [and] horrible slaughter," Glatthaar wrote.

In the end, 5,000 Union soldiers lost their lives at the Battle of the Crater. The 29th U.S. Colored Infantry entered the fight with 450 troops and left with just 128. More than 40 percent of the deaths that day were in black commands, in spite of the fact that most soldiers who fought were white. (The black soldier's high death rate occurred because of Rebel refusal to take black prisoners. Confederates instead would kill them outright.) The siege of Petersburg would have to continue. Though they fought courageously, black soldiers would have to wait another day to avenge Fort Pillow.

VALOR APLENTY

Throughout the four years of the Civil War, African-American troops fought in 449 engagements, 39 of which were major battles. Congressional Medals of Honor were awarded to 17 soldiers and 4 naval seamen.

It is not argued that black soldiers fought with bravery, and they did so despite the fact that they came later to the battle than their white counterparts, with less training and experience to bring against an experienced Confederate army. Furthermore, as reported in *Forged in Battle*, "Most high-ranking Union officers preferred to use black troops for fatigue and noncombat duty and rely on the veteran white commands for combat. Thus, black units had little time for drill and were often relegated to rear-area occupation duties or secondary and tertiary campaigns." That said, in the closing year of the war, African-American soldiers still found plenty of action and had many opportunities to show valor and fortitude.

In South Carolina, the 7th U.S. Colored Infantry literally rescued a veteran white regiment that had run out of ammunition. "As the black troops marched in behind the line, veteran white soldiers broke and fled under the weight of a Confederate assault," Joseph Glatthaar reported. "The men of the 7th U.S. Colored Infantry turned toward the Confederates and advanced boldly, with white Federal troops pouring through their formation, and filled the gap in the Federal line to repulse the attack."

At Chaffin's Farm, on September 29 and 30, 1864, black soldiers suffered huge losses charging over difficult ground against a strong Confederate fortification. One company lost 87 percent of its men in the assault. One entire regiment experienced 209 casualties out of 377 who were engaged. Still, the unit's brigade commander, himself among the wounded, was reported to have cried out, as quoted in *Forged in Battle*, "Ah! Give me the Thunder-heads & Black hearts after all. They fought splendidly that morning, facing the red tempest of death with unflinching heroism."

The 5th U.S Colored Cavalry, on its way to Saltville, silently endured the insults and harassment of white Northern volunteers as they marched by. The whites insulted the cavalry's lack of combat experience and fighting skill. In the battle to come, the Confederates would kill 118 of the 400 black soldiers. Yet the Federal troops were able to get deep into Rebel territory. On their return, white troops who had scoffed at their "black brothers" stood in silent respect for what had been accomplished.

Few people know that many other African Americans saw action in the Civil War not as soldiers, but rather as seamen in the United States Navy. It is estimated that 18,000 served in this way (though some historians consider that figure exaggerated). "While the Negro soldier was proving his mettle, the Negro sailor was going unobtrusively ahead in his service to the country," reported Benjamin Quarles, in *The Negro in the Civil War*. "Throughout its history, the navy had never barred free Negroes from enlisting, and in September 1861 it had adopted the policy of signing up former slaves." Eventually, a quarter of the men sailing the Union fleet during the Civil War perhaps were black.

Although history often recounts the contributions of black soldiers during the Civil War, black sailors (above) also sacrificed a great deal during the tumultuous era. The U.S. Navy had always welcomed free blacks and actively recruited former slaves in 1861 to join their ranks. Allowed to eat and sleep along with the other crew members, these new sailors were treated better than the soldiers who served on land.

At the end of 1864, the federal government issued orders giving permission for the formation of the 25th United States Army Corps. The corps was to be the only one in the country's history to be made up almost entirely of black infantry regiments—30 in all. In late 1864, a final Union victory dawned. The African-American soldier had found a place in an army that now not only accepted him, but also desperately needed his services to bring the Civil War to its bitter conclusion.

WAR'S END

The Confederate cause had become hopeless by April 1865, if not sooner. General Robert E. Lee still had his army, beaten as

Jim Crow Laws

The Jim Crow laws of the South, in effect, made segregation a legal government action. They were named after "Jump Jim Crow," a song-and-dance caricature of African Americans from the early nineteenth-century. The laws were enforced between 1876 and the mid-twentieth century throughout the South and border states, mandating a "separate but equal" status for black Americans. In reality, the rights afforded blacks were always inferior to those provided to whites. Jim Crow legalized segregation.

Below are some examples of Jim Crow laws as they applied to marriage, public facilities, education, entertainment, and free speech.

Marriage
"All marriages between a white person and a Negro, or between a white person and a person of Negro descent to the fourth generation inclusive, are hereby forever prohibited." (Florida)

Public Facilities
"It shall be unlawful for a Negro and white person to play together or in company with each other at any game of pool or billiards." (Alabama)

it was, but he could no longer take the offensive. Survival became his only concern. In the first days of April, the general abandoned Richmond and fled west in a forced march. Confederate president Jefferson Davis headed southward, hoping to find refuge in North Carolina, where he might continue to command—but the war, in effect, was over.

On April 4, President Lincoln decided to pay a visit to captured Richmond. When he arrived, the only people in the area

"No colored barber shall serve as a barber to white women or girls." (Georgia)

Education

"The schools for white children and the schools for Negro children shall be conducted separately." (Florida)

Entertainment

"All circuses, shows, and tent exhibitions, to which the attendance of . . . more than one race is invited or expected to attend shall provide for the convenience of its patrons not less than two ticket offices with individual ticket sellers, and not less than two entrances to the said performance, with individual ticket takers and receivers, and in the case of outside or tent performances, the said ticket offices shall not be less than twenty-five feet apart." (Louisiana)

Free Speech

"Any person . . . who shall be guilty of printing, publishing or circulating printed, typewritten or written material urging or presenting for public acceptance or general information, arguments or suggestions in favor of social equality or of intermarriage between whites and Negroes, shall be guilty of a misdemeanor and subject to fine of not exceeding five hundred dollars or imprisonment not exceeding six months or both." (Mississippi)

Source: Jessica McElrath, *African-American History*, About.com.

were a group of 40 African-American laborers. One of them, a 60-year-old man, recognized the bearded man in the tall black hat. The laborer sprang forward and cried out, as quoted in *The Negro in the Civil War*, "Bress de Lord, dere is de great Messiah! I knowed him as soon as I seed him. He's ben in my heart fo' yeahs an' he's cum at las' to free his chillum from deir bondage! Glory, hallelujah!" In no time, the streets of Richmond were alive with black faces.

General Lee and his battered army made it west as far as Appomattox Court House. On April 9, Lee surrendered to Union forces in a dignified ceremony free from ill will. Black troops were there to help celebrate the surrender.

On April 14, four years after the war had begun, the Union flag was again raised over Fort Sumter in Charleston Harbor. Abolitionist William Lloyd Garrison was there, and so was Robert Smalls, piloting the flag-bedecked steamer the *Planter*. According to Eric Foner in his book *Reconstruction*, "Smalls was so overcome by emotion that he lost his bearings, and the ship collided with another during the ceremony." April 14, 1865, was indeed a great day for the Union. The night, however, was something else.

President Lincoln knew full well that the Union had triumphed and the war for reunification and emancipation had been won. Lincoln decided to relax from all his tensions by taking in a play at Ford's Theatre. On the very day the war all but ended, the president of the United States was murdered while he sat in his box seat. "For the first time in [American children's] lives," reported James Marten in *Children for the Union*, "they saw grown men crying in public."

No group felt more hurt and saddened at the president's assassination than African Americans. "We at first could not comprehend it," one officer of the Massachusetts 54th wrote in shock, as quoted in *A Voice of Thunder*. "It was too overwhelming, too lamentable, too distressing."

In the months and years to come, African Americans would have reason enough to mourn the early death of the nation's sixteenth president. Through his policies, tardy as some may have been, Lincoln did more than any one individual to bring freedom to four million previously enslaved Americans. That said, however, there is little question that those same black Americans owed that very freedom as much to their own efforts during the Civil War as to any white man who fought for and beside them.

FREE AT LAST! FREE AT LAST!

August 23, 1963, was a sweltering day, typical of Washington, D.C., in the summertime. Yet still they came, 200,000-strong, to fill the capital's National Mall, stretching from the Lincoln Memorial back as far as the halls of Congress.

As part of the March on Washington for Jobs and Freedom, civil rights leader Martin Luther King Jr. would deliver the main speech. The speech was guaranteed to be the march's main event, one that sought not only to summarize the injustice faced by African Americans, but also to call for a uniting of all Americans. It would be a cry to finally bring the full promise of emancipation to African Americans that had been promised a hundred years earlier. In that effort, listeners would not be disappointed.

It is not known what, exactly, King's thoughts were that day as he approached the podium, with the large, white Georgia marble statue of the Great Emancipator, Abraham Lincoln, just a few yards behind him. One thing is clear, however: King knew well enough that in the century since the Civil War, African Americans had suffered terribly. Decade after decade, they saw their hopes for equality and social acceptance turned away countless times.

Perhaps King recalled to himself the failure of Reconstruction, the federal government's plan from 1863 to 1877 to uplift the freed slave and force the South to follow new Constitutional amendments guaranteeing his freedom, his citizenship, and his right to vote.

Perhaps King mourned the full-scale segregation of the late-nineteenth century that placed the infamous "separate but equal" Jim Crow laws throughout the South. Many of these laws were still in effect as King prepared to speak.

Perhaps the civil rights leader shuddered as he pictured the terror of the Ku Klux Klan, Black Legion, Silver Shirts, and other hate groups that attempted to keep blacks down, to force them to "know their place."

Perhaps King recalled his own struggles in confronting many white Southerners who so strongly believed that whites were superior and that white supremacy was God's will.

Perhaps King knew only too well that the South had for far too long been celebrating the peace, though the North had won the Civil War a century earlier. His plea, to be known from that point as his "I have a dream" speech, was designed to set in motion forces that would right that long century of injustice and abuse.

King told his audience, in his slow, powerful voice, as quoted on the United States Department of State Web site:

> In a sense we've come to our nation's capital to cash a
> check. When the architects of our republic wrote the
> magnificent words of the Constitution and the Declara-
> tion of Independence, they were signing a promissory note
> to which every American was to fall heir. This note was a
> promise that all men, yes, black men as well as white men,
> would be guaranteed the unalienable rights of life,
> liberty and the pursuit of happiness.

King then went on to declare:

> I have a dream that one day this nation will rise up and
> live out the true meaning of its creed: "We hold these truths
> to be self-evident, that all men are created equal." I have a
> dream that one day on the red hills of Georgia, the sons of
> former slaves and the sons of former slave owners will be

able to sit down together at the table of brotherhood. . . .
I have a dream that my four little children will one day
live in a nation where they will not be judged by the color
of their skin but by the content of their character.

Then, raising his deep voice to its full power, his right arm out-stretched, Martin Luther King Jr. concluded:

From every mountainside, let freedom ring.

And when this happens, when we allow freedom to ring,
when we let it ring from every village and every hamlet,
from every state and every city, we will be able to speed
up that day when all of God's children, black men and
white men, Jews and Gentiles, Protestants and Catholics,
will be able to join hands and sing in the words of the
old Negro spiritual:

Free at last! Free at last!
Thank God Almighty, we are free at last!

Glossary

ARMY A military unit consisting of about 16,000 men, or two or more corps.

BATTERY A grouping of artillery pieces, as in a fortification.

BORDER STATES Refers to the five slave states of Delaware, Kentucky, Maryland, Missouri, and West Virginia that stayed with the Union during the Civil War.

BRIGADE A military unit consisting of about 2,000 men, or two or more regiments.

BUREAU OF COLORED TROOPS A federal government agency, set up on May 22, 1863, the function of which was to embrace all matters pertaining to the recruitment, organization, and service of black regiments and their officers.

CHATTEL An item, usually movable, connected with real property; a slave was considered to be such property.

COMMISSIONED OFFICER An officer of the armed services holding, by a commission, a rank of second lieutenant, ensign, or above.

COMPANY A military unit usually consisting of 100 men.

CONFISCATION ACT An act passed by the federal government on July 17, 1862, which declared free the slaves of all who were in rebellion.

CONSCRIPTED Enrolled into the military by force; drafted.

CONTRABAND Enemy goods taken in wartime; contraband included a slave who, during the Civil War, escaped to or was brought within the Union lines.

CORPS A military unit consisting of about 8,000 men, or two or more divisions.

DIVISION   A military unit consisting of about 4,000 men, or two or more brigades.

DRAFTED   To be selected for military service.

DRILL   To train or exercise in the military in preparation for battle or parade.

EMBEDDED   A non-military person, usually a news reporter, placed with a fighting unit.

ENLISTEE   A man in a Civil War army, ranking below a commissioned or warrant officer.

FLOTILLA   A fleet of ships.

INSURRECTION   An act or instance of revolting against civil authority or an established government.

MANEUVERS   An armed-forces training exercise.

MARTIAL LAW   The law administered by military forces that is invoked by a government in an emergency when the civilian law enforcement agencies are unable to maintain public order and safety.

MARTYR   A person who sacrifices something of great value, especially his or her life, for the sake of principle.

METTLE   Staying-quality, stamina, spirit.

NEGRO   The term once used to refer to people who belonged to the black race.

NONCOMMISSIONED OFFICER   A subordinate officer (as a sergeant) in the army appointed from among the enlisted ranks.

PALMETTO   Any of several low-growing, fan-leaved palms, the trunks of which are quite strong.

PLATOON   A military unit consisting of 50 men, or five squads.

REGIMENT   A military unit consisting of about 1,000 men, or 10 companies.

SLAVER   A ship used in the slave trade.

SQUAD   A military unit consisting of 10 to 12 men.

TERTIARY CAMPAIGN   A military action of third-rank importance or value.

TO THE FLAG   Seeking the safety of a fort or other protective unit of organization.

WHITE SUPREMACY   The doctrine based on a belief in the inherent superiority of the white race over other races, necessitating the subordination of nonwhites to whites in all relationships.

Bibliography

AfricanAmericans.com. "Fighting for Freedom: Black Union Soldiers of the Civil War." Available online. URL: http://www.africanamericans.com/BlackUnionSoldiersCivilWar.htm. Accessed November 24, 2008.

Africans in America: America's Journey Through Slavery. Part I, 1450–1760—The Terrible Transformation. WBGH, 1998.

Allen, Thomas. *The Blue and the Gray*. Washington, D.C.: National Geographic Society, 1992.

The American Civil War. Available online. URL: http://www.us-civilwar.com/-2k. Accessed November 24, 2008.

The Arkansas News. Available online. URL: http://www.oldstatehouse.com. Accessed November 24, 2008.

Bennett, James Gordon. *New York Herald*, October 20, 1862.

Berlin, Ira, Joseph Reidy, and Leslie Rowland, eds. *Freedom's Soldiers: The Black Military Experience in the Civil War*. New York: Cambridge University Press, 1998.

Blight, David. *A Slave No More: Two Men Who Escaped to Freedom*. New York: Harcourt, 2007.

Burchard, Peter. *One Gallant Rush: Robert Gould Shaw & His Brave Black Regiment*. New York: St. Martin's Press, 1965.

Burns, Ken. *The Civil War*, PBS Paramount. 1990.

Catton, Bruce. *The Civil War*. Boston: Houghton Mifflin Company, 2005.

"The Civil War." Available online. URL: http://members.aol.com/TeacherNet/civilwar.html. Accessed November 24, 2008.

Darman, Peter. *Civil War Trivia Book*. New York: Barnes & Noble Books, 2007.

Davis, Burke. *The Civil War, Strange and Fascinating Facts*. New York: Barnes and Noble, 1995.

Davis, George. *The Official Military Atlas of the Civil War*. New York: Barnes & Noble Books, 1983.

Douglass, Frederick. *Narrative of the Life of Frederick Douglass, an American Slave*. New York: Barnes & Noble Classics, 2003.

EyeWitness to History. "Aboard a Slave Ship, 1829." Available online. URL: http://www.eyewitnesstohistory.com. Accessed November 24, 2008.

EyeWitness to History. "Slave Auction, 1959." Available online. URL: http://www.eyewitnesstohistory.com. Accessed November 24, 2008.

FamilyEducation.com. "African American Troops in the Civil War." Available online. URL: http://school.familyeducation.com/african-american-history/us-civil-war/47432.html. Accessed November 24, 2008.

Farrow, Anne, Joel Lang, and Jenifer Frank. *Complicity: How the North Promoted, Prolonged, and Profited from Slavery*. New York: Ballantine Books, 2006.

Foner, Eric. *Reconstruction: America's Unfinished Revolution*. New York: Perennial Classics, 1989.

Foote, Shelby. *The Civil War: A Narrative*. New York: Random House, 1958.

Gilmore, Glenda Elizabeth. *Defying Dixie: The Radical Roots of Civil Rights*. New York: W.W. Norton & Company, 2008.

Glatthaar, Joseph. *Forged in Battle: The Civil War Alliance of Black Soldiers and White Officers*. Baton Rouge: Louisiana State University Press, 1990.

Gutman, Herbert. *The Black Family in Slavery & Freedom, 1750–1925*. New York: Pantheon Books, 1976.

Hollandsworth, James. *The Louisiana Native Guards: The Black Military Experience During the Civil War*. Baton Rouge: Louisiana State University Press, 1995.

Joyner, Charles. *Down by the Riverside: A South Carolina Slave Community*. Urbana-Champaign: University of Illinois Press, 1984.

Klingaman, William. *Abraham Lincoln and the Road to Emancipation*. New York: Viking, 2001.

Library of Congress. "Photographs of African Americans During the Civil War: A List of Images in the Civil War Photograph Collection." Available online. URL: http://www.loc.gov/rr/print/list/081_cwaf.html. Accessed November 24, 2008.

———. "Pre–Civil War African-American Slavery." Available online. URL: http://memory.loc.gov/learn/features/timeline/expref/slavery/slavery.html. Accessed November 24, 2008.

Lockett, James. "The Lynching Massacre of Black and White Soldiers at Fort Pillow, Tennessee, April 12, 1864." *The Western Journal of Black Studies*, Vol. 22, 1998.

Long Island University. "The African American: A Journey from Slavery to Freedom." Available online. URL: http://www.liu.edu/cwis/cwp/library/aaslavry.htm. Accessed November 24, 2008.

Marten, James. *Children for the Union: The War Spirit on the Northern Home Front*. Chicago: Ivan R. Dee, 2004.

McCague, James. *The Second Rebellion: The New York City Draft Riots of 1863*. New York: The Dial Press, 1968.

McPherson, James. *The Negro's Civil War*. New York: Random House, 1993.

Morris, Roy. *The Long Pursuit: Abraham Lincoln's Thirty-Year Struggle with Stephen Douglas for the Heart and Soul of America*. New York: HarperCollins, 2008.

National Park Service. "African-American Civil War Sailors." Available online. URL: http://www.civilwar.nps.gov/cwss/partners_aasailors.htm. Accessed November 24, 2008.

———. "History of African Americans in the Civil War." Available online. URL: http://www.itd.nps.gov/cwss/history/aa_history.htm. Accessed November 24, 2008.

Office American Freedmen's Inquiry Commission. *Preliminary Report*. New York: Secretary of War, 1863.

———. *Final Report*. New York: Secretary of War, 1864.

Quarles, Benjamin. *The Negro in the Civil War*. New York: DaCapo Press, 1989.

Redkey, Edwin, ed. *A Grand Army of Black Men*. New York: Cambridge University Press, 1992.

Shotgun's Home of the American Civil War. "John Charles Fremont, 1813–1890." Available online. URL: http://www.civilwarhome.com/fremontbio.htm. Accessed November 24, 2008.

Stowe, Harriet Beecher. *Uncle Tom's Cabin*. New York: Barnes & Noble Classics, 1852.

Taylor, Susie King. *A Black Woman's Civil War Memoirs.* Princeton, N.J.: Markus Wiener Publishers, 1988.

Thomas, Hugh. *The Slave Trade: The Story of the Atlantic Slave Trade, 1440–1870.* New York: Simon & Schuster, 1997.

United States Colored Troops: Civil War. Available online. URL: http://www.coax.net/people/lwf/usct.htm. Accessed November 24, 2008.

United States Department of State. "Text of 'I Have a Dream' Speech." Available online. URL: http://usinfo.state.gov/infousa/government/overview/38.html. Accessed November 24, 2008.

United States History. "The Abolitionists." Available online. URL: http://countrystudies.us/united-states/history-59.htm. Accessed November 24, 2008.

University of Maryland. "Freedom and Southern Society Project." Available online. URL: http://www.history.umd.edu/Freeddmen/fssphome.htm. Accessed November 24, 2008.

University of Washington Libraries. "African-American History." Available online. URL: http://www.lib.washington.edu/subject/History/tm/black.html. Accessed November 24, 2008.

World History Archives. "African-American History Before the Civil War." Available online. URL: http://www.hartford-hwp.com/archives/45a/index-h.html. Accessed November 24, 2008.

Yacovone, Donald. *A Voice of Thunder: A Black Soldier's Civil War.* Chicago: University of Illinois Press, 1998.

NEWSPAPER ARTICLES

"A Negro Riot in Harrisburgh." *New York Times,* May 31, 1863.

"Exemption Ordinance." *New York Times,* August 29, 1963.

"Explanations Regarding the Draft." *New York Times,* July 14, 1863.

New York Daily Tribune, March 9, 1859.

New York Tribune, September 19, 1865.

"News from Washington." *New York Times,* December 25, 1863.

"The Port Hudson Heroes." *New York Times,* June 13, 1863.

Richmond Examiner, July 19, 1863.

"The Riots in This City." *New York Times,* July 22, 1863.

Further Resources

Black, Wallace. *Slaves to Soldiers: African-American Fighting Men in the Civil War*. London: Franklin Watts, 1998.

Cartmell, Donald. *Civil War 101: Everything You Ever Wanted to Know About the North, the South, the Leaders, the Battles, and the History*. New York: Gramercy, 2004.

Fuller, James. *Men of Color, To Arms!* San Jose, Calif.: University Press, 2001.

Grant, Callie. *Janie's Freedom: African Americans in the Aftermath of the Civil War (1867)*. Uhrichsville, Ohio: Barbour Publishing, 2006.

Green, Carl, and William Saford. *Union Generals of the Civil War*. Berkeley Heights, N.J.: Enslow Publishers, 1998.

Haskins, Jim. *Black, Blue & Gray: African Americans in the Civil War*. New York: Simon & Schuster Children's Publishing, 1998.

Mattern, Joanne. *The Big Book of the Civil War: Fascinating Facts About the Civil War, Including Historic Photographs, Maps, and Documents*. New York: Courage Books, 2007.

Rosoff, Iris, ed. *Civil War*. New York: Kindersley, 2000.

Vaughan, Donald. *The Everything Civil War Book*. Holbrook, Mass.: Adams Media Corporation, 2000.

WEB SITES

African-American Civil War Memorial Freedom Foundation and Museum
http://www.afroamcivilwar.org

African-American Freedom Fighters: Soldiers of Liberty
http://www.liu.edu/cwis/cwp/library/aaffsfl.htm

Africa-American Medal of Honor Winners from the Civil War to the Spanish American War
http://www.liu.edu/cwis/cwp/library/aaslavry.htm

Africans in America
http://www.pbs.org/wgbh/aia/part1/narrative.html

Frederick Douglass: American Abolitionist
http://americancivilwar.com/colored/frederick_douglass.html

Gettysburg National Military Park
http://www.nps.gov/archive/gett/gettour/armorg.htm

Picture Credits

Index

About the Authors

RONALD A. REIS is the author of 18 books, including *The Dust Bowl*, *The Empire State Building*, and *The New York Subway System*.

TIM MCNEESE is associate professor of history at York College in York, Nebraska, where he is in his seventeenth year of college instruction. Professor McNeese earned an associate of arts degree from York College, a bachelor of arts in history and political science from Harding University, and a master of arts in history from Missouri State University. A prolific author of books for elementary, middle and high school, and college readers, McNeese has published more than 100 books and educational materials over the past 20 years, on everything from the founding of early New York to Hispanic authors. His writing has earned him a citation in the library reference work *Contemporary Authors* and multiple citations in *Best Books for Young Teen Readers*. In 2006, McNeese appeared on the History Channel program *Risk Takers, History Makers: John Wesley Powell and the Grand Canyon*. He was a faculty member at the 2006 Tony Hillerman Writers Conference in Albuquerque. His wife, Beverly, is an assistant professor of English at York College. They have two married children, Noah and Summer, and three grandchildren, Ethan, Adrianna, and Finn William. Tim and Bev McNeese sponsored study trips for college students on the Lewis and Clark Trail in 2003 and 2005 and to the American Southwest in 2008. You may contact Professor McNeese at tdmcneese@york.edu.

BL

BLYDEN BRANCH
Norfolk Public Library